The E-Primer

The E-Primer

An introduction to creating
psychological experiments in E-Prime®

Michiel Spapé
Rinus Verdonschot
Saskia van Dantzig
Henk van Steenbergen

LEIDEN UNIVERSITY PRESS

Cover design: Mulder van Meurs, Amsterdam
Lay-out: V3-Services, Baarn

ISBN   978 90 8728 183 0
E-ISBN   978 94 0060 129 1
NUR   770/980

Acknowledgements

This book is the result of intensive collaboration between people who, at one time or another, studied or worked at Leiden University. In 2006, we extended a collection of E-Prime exercises into something resembling a coherent course. In subsequent years, we – initially as a rather dynamic collective of PhD students – have revised the manual in order to help those who want to prepare for creating their own psychological experiments. Later, we expanded the work so it can now also serve as a basic introduction to E-Basic coding in E-Prime.

Along the way, many people helped us in the writing of this book. First, we would like to thank David McFarlane, Michael Richter, Kerstin Brinkmann and the people at Psychology Software Tools for providing helpful comments when reviewing an earlier draft of this book. There were also numerous students who provided useful feedback during the period when this book was being used for courses at Leiden University. In particular, we would like to thank Hans Revers and Erwin Haasnoot for their constructive comments. Many more people have joined our journey, but at different moments in time. Each of us would like to mention a few:

Michiel Spapé: "I would like to thank Elkan Akyürek for introducing me to E-Prime and Jan-Rouke Kuipers for sharing my "pain" as we first started to teach it ourselves. Stephan Verschoor for being my favourite "unhappy victim" for demonstration purposes when no student volunteered – the nightmare of any teacher. Wido la Heij and Gezinus Wolters for providing my mind with many brilliant exemplars in teaching: easily retrieved from memory, yet so hard to successfully imitate, and Zania Sovijärvi-Spapé, for continuing to put up with a coding geek."

Rinus Verdonschot: "I am grateful to the Cognitive Psychology department of Leiden University for giving me the chance to teach E-prime to so many enthusiastic students and also to the people who participate actively in the Google E-Prime group and, thus, help out researchers all over the world. Lastly, a big thanks to my family, friends and colleagues."

Saskia van Dantzig: "I'd like to thank Diane Pecher, who introduced me to E-Prime and encouraged me to develop the E-Prime course for psychology students at the Erasmus University. This course supplemented several chapters of this book. Diane was also one of the reviewers of this book. Thanks to Rolf Zwaan for challenging me to program complicated experiments, which boosted my programming skills and let me explore the endless possibilities of E-Prime. Thanks to my former colleagues at Leiden University and Erasmus University. To conclude, thanks to Alexander for his encouragement and to my kids for enabling me to do the work I love. "

Henk van Steenbergen: "I would like to thank the many colleagues at Leiden University with whom I have been sharing E-Prime problems and solutions on a daily or weekly basis. Thanks to Guido Band, Bernhard Hommel and Sander Nieuwenhuis for encouraging me to publish this book. Thanks to Belle Derks for helping us to set up the revised E-Prime course, and Margot Schel for helping me to thoroughly revise and extend the predecessor of this book, resulting in the current end product. Anne Bolders provided great help with proof-reading. Thanks to Thijs Schrama for providing technical help along the way. Finally, I am grateful to Eveline and my family and friends for encouraging me to get this book published."

Table of Contents

Introduction

The E-Primer is written with a reader in mind who is eager to learn, but knows little, *if anything*, about programming, computer science and the actual implementation of all those wonderful scientific experiments that make up the body of the reading list of psychologists and cognitive scientists. This is not to say, however, that more experienced readers will not find it interesting as many chapters also deal with advanced E-Prime® and programming skills.

What is E-Prime® and what will I learn?

E-Prime® is a software package used to design and run psychological experiments, with a focus on psychological and cognitive science, and to acquire and analyse data. E-Prime® consists of a number of programs with different functions. In The E-Primer, we will discuss *E-Studio, E-Basic, E-Merge, E-Recovery* and *E-DataAid*. We will assume you use E-Prime 2, but most of the features we discuss were already introduced in E-Prime 1. When the two versions significantly differ in operation, we discuss each separately.

You will learn how to use each of these programs effectively in order to ultimately implement your very own experiments. First, however, you will learn how to re-create a number of fascinating, famous experiments. We guide you through this process in an easy to follow, step-by-step approach – 'now click on this button over there' – using *Tutorials*. Along the way, we explain why this is being done and try to communicate our insights on general good practice in design. Gradually, we will move beyond the narrow confines of the 'click-here-now-there' steps and ask you to implement simple variations. These form the basis of the *Exercises* at the end of each chapter. Finally, in the *Advanced exercises* you will be asked to explore, with minimal guidance, the horizons of E-Prime® and how you could pursue the effective realisation of your own research interests. Make sure that you save your work, because you may need it in subsequent chapters.

Why should I learn E-Prime®?

There are a number of reasons to learn E-Prime®. First, many students during their studies will become involved in doing a research project. This will eventually involve setting up and programming an experiment, which requires good E-Prime® programming skills.

Second, learning to program is more than just learning a specific programming language. Programming involves mostly logical thinking. Once you have learned to program in E-Prime®, you can easily transfer your knowledge and skills to new programming languages. Moreover, you will have learned to think about experiments in a structured and logical way. This skill is not only useful for setting up an experiment yourself (for example, during your research project), but it also helps you to read and understand empirical papers. Finally, we hope we can communicate some of our own enthusiasm and the idea that programming and realising your imagination, creating something out of nothing, is really a lot of fun.

Online support

E-Prime® has a good support website: *http://www.pstnet.com/support/login.asp*. Here, you will find examples of experiments and answers to frequently asked questions and problems. If you encounter a problem and can't find the answer on their FAQ and knowledge-base pages, you can send them your question via a special form on the website. You will then receive a personal answer, usually within a day or two. In order to get this personal support, you have to register (for free) on the website.

More information can also be found in the E-Prime® manuals. There is a short 'Getting Started Guide' and a more extensive 'User's Guide' and 'Reference Guide' (Schneider, Eschman, & Zuccolotto, 2002).You can also find more information on the STEP (System for Teaching Experimental Psychology) website. STEP is a web-based project designed to maximize the use of E-Prime®: *http://step.psy.cmu.edu/*.

This website includes ample examples of common paradigms in experimental psychology. It should be noted that these experiments are programmed in the previous version of E-Prime® (E-Prime 1). However, you can still open and run these experiments in the current E-Prime® version (E-Prime 2).

Lastly, an independently-run mailing list exists with a sizeable community that may be able to assist with urgent queries that simply can't wait for the E-Prime® support. Or, perhaps you have a more design-related question, or just want to let everyone know how much you love designing experiments in E-Prime®: *http://groups.google.com/group/e-prime*.

Chapter I

E-Prime® at a glance

In this chapter, you will learn

About: • E-Studio, E-DataAid, E-Recovery and E-Merge
• Object Oriented Programming
• E-Studio's structure
• Procedures
• Lists
• TextDisplays

How to: • Create your first experiment
• Pimp your experiment
• Save and analyse your data

This chapter will introduce you to the E-Prime® software package. You will get acquainted with the different programs that enable you to create, run and analyse experiments. You will learn that E-Prime® uses **object oriented programming** to offer you different types of objects. These E-Objects function as building blocks that enable you to create your own experiments in a relatively simple and straightforward way. Before actually starting to program, it is important to visualise what your experiment will look like. Firstly, you will learn how to conceptualise your experiment, which makes the actual programming a lot easier. After reading this chapter, you should be able to program, run and analyse your own first experiment.

E-Studio, E-DataAid, E-Recovery and E-Merge

When we talk about 'working in E-Prime®', 'an experiment written in E-Prime®', or even 'E-Prime® crashed again', we generally mean E-Studio. You may be delighted – or disheartened – to learn that E-Prime® is actually a software package composed of a number of programs other than E-Studio. We will talk about these other programs throughout this book, but, generally, they are straightforward and don't merit coverage beyond a quick summary.

E-Studio is based on, or perhaps merely inspired by, Visual Studio and can be called an 'IDE: an integrated development environment'. The graphical user interface is a convenient way to write (*develop*) code, simply by dragging and dropping objects onto a timeline. This makes the daunting task of developing experiments at least *look* as simple as using friendly and familiar Windows programs like PowerPoint. However, it is not quite true that no real programming (i.e. *coding* or *scripting*) is required: almost all original experiments at some point require the developer to write at least a few lines of code; and, more importantly, it can save a lot of time to do so. We will see how this works in later chapters. The experiment in E-Studio is stored as an **.es2** file.

E-DataAid is a program that can read E-Prime® output. Whenever an E-Prime® experiment is run, a unique datafile is created (an **.edat2** file). These .edat2 files can't be opened directly by Microsoft Excel or SPSS, but you can use E-DataAid to convert them into such formats. Additionally, E-DataAid comes with many additional features that make it much easier to get your data in proper shape for analysis. For example, you can filter out missing data before exporting, explore outliers and filter them out, generate crosstabs to base your graphs on, etc.

E-Merge does nothing more than merge data. Typically, when you have run *N* subjects, you will end up with *N* .edat2 datafiles. Of course, you can analyse each one in turn, or even import each one into SPSS, but this involves the risk that each action can go wrong, adding a chance of data-corruption due to human- or machine error; furthermore, each action costs time. With E-Merge you can merge the *N* datafiles into one large file. To merge a set of datafiles, take the following steps:

1. find the .edat2 files that your experiment has generated;
2. select them all using your mouse and control- or shift-clicking;
3. click on the *Merge* button.

This generates a **.emrg2** file, which can also be opened and analysed within E-DataAid.

E-Recovery is the smallest and simplest program in the package. If E-Prime® crashes during an experiment, no .edat2 file is generated. However, when the experiment is running (aka. runtime), a **.txt file** is created to which data from each trial are appended. This .txt file contains the same data as the .edat2 file, but it is rather inconvenient to analyse. So, should E-Prime® crash after having gone through several trials, you can open E-Recovery and take the following steps to recover the (partial) data:

1. press *Browse*;
2. look up the specific .txt file that you wish to recover;
3. press *Recover*.

Now you have an .edat2 file that is fully equivalent to the others, except that it lacks a few trials (if you are lucky). Since this is all E-Recovery does, the program will not be mentioned anywhere else in this book.

E-Run allows you to run experiments. When you have created an experiment in E-Studio and press *(control+) F7*, an **.ebs2** (encrypted e-basic script) file is created. The .ebs2 file can be run in E-Run.

Object Oriented Programming

E-Prime®, like many popular programming languages such as C# and Visual Basic .NET, is based on the concept of **Object Oriented Programming** (OOP).

A good example of an **object** in daily life is 'a car'. One can do certain things with objects, such as *driving, steering* and *pursuing horizons*. In programming, we call such abilities **methods**. In programming script, an object's method is indicated in the following way: Object.method(parameters). For example, the code Car.drive(forward) would let the car object drive forward, the *Car* being the object, *drive* being the method, *forward* being a parameter of the *drive*-method. The other important feature of objects is that they usually have **properties**: a car can *be red, has a top speed of 200 km/h, has four seats* and so on. If we wanted to tell an object oriented programming language that our car is dark blue, we would say that our *Car.colour = dark blue, car* being the object, *colour* being the property and *dark blue* being the parameter of the colour property.

From idea to result

Designing, running and analysing an experiment with E-Prime software

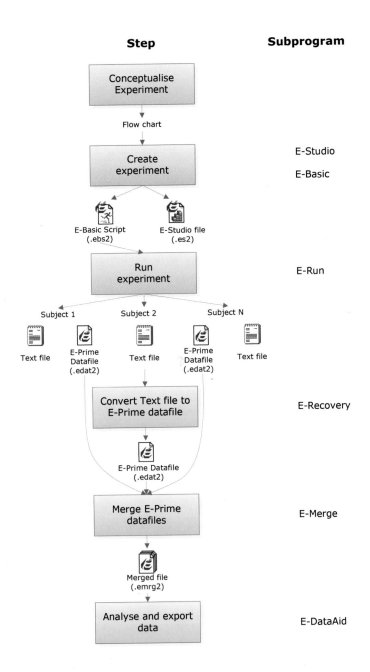

Step	Subprogram

Conceptualise Experiment

Flow chart

Create experiment — E-Studio / E-Basic

E-Basic Script (.ebs2) E-Studio file (.es2)

Run experiment — E-Run

Subject 1 Subject 2 Subject N

Text file E-Prime Datafile (.edat2) Text file E-Prime Datafile (.edat2) Text file

Convert Text file to E-Prime datafile — E-Recovery

E-Prime Datafile (.edat2)

Merge E-Prime datafiles — E-Merge

Merged file (.emrg2)

Analyse and export data — E-DataAid

Two other concepts of OOP are *instances* and *inheritance*. Our car, for example, is not just any car, it is OUR car! That is to say, *ourCar* is an **instance**;, in other words, a particular or token from the object or type *Car*. This matters for programming, because if we add something to *myCar*, such as a boom-box or mirror dice, this does not alter cars in general, but the same is not true if cars in general come equipped with such devices. **Inheritance** is also about the types and tokens: since our car is a Suzuki, it *inherits* certain properties and methods that are generally true for most cars, such as that it comes with a steering wheel and four wheels. Specifically, our car is a Suzuki Swift, which inherits certain features from the Suzuki object, such as its cheap price and uncomfortable seats.

Don't worry if these concepts strike you as difficult and abstract. Understanding them is not crucial to programming basic experiments, but since they are of such importance to modern-day programming, we hope that their functions will be revealed to you during your work with E-Prime®.

Conceptualising an experiment

When you are designing an experiment you might be tempted to run to your computer and start programming straight away. However, before you start programming, you should try to visualise what your experiment will look like. This may sound self-evident, but it remains an important step that is easily omitted, with nasty, if not fatal, consequences ensuing. So, try to conceptualise the experiment by asking yourself the following questions:

- What kind of design do you need? A between-subjects design or a within-subjects design?
- Which variables do you manipulate? In other words, what are the independent variables? How many levels do these variables have? How many conditions does the experiment have?
- What are the dependent variables that you will measure? For example, do you aquire data regarding reaction time, error rates, and so on?
- Does your experiment contain blocks of trials? If yes, what is the order of presentation of these blocks?
- Does your experiment have a practice block?
- How do you instruct the participant?
- What happens during a trial? What kind of stimulus is presented? How long is the stimulus presented for? How should the participant respond? What happens if the participant responds too slowly?

- What happens between trials? Does the participant get feedback? How long is the interval between trials (we call this the **inter-trial interval, ITI**)?
- In which order are trials presented? In random order? In a fixed order? Or in a semi-random order?

To facilitate programming, it can be useful to draw a flow chart that displays the structure of the experiment. An experiment typically contains a hierarchy of Procedures. The main Procedure (called 'SessionProc' in E-Prime®) determines the global order of events in the experiment. This one is depicted on the left. Sub-Procedures are depicted to the right of the main Procedure. A flow chart contains different elements:

A flow chart contains different elements:

Event: Refers to a specific event during the experiment, for example the presentation of a picture, text or sound. Indicates what happens, the duration of the event, and how the event is terminated (e.g. by pressing the *space bar*).

Sub procedure: Refers to a Procedure at a lower level of the hierarchy. Indicates the name of the Procedure, the number of repetitions of the Procedure and the order of the repetitions (e.g. random).

Decision: The Procedure branches into two options. The diamond indicates a criterion (e.g. response = correct, or reaction time < 1000). If the criterion is met, the Yes-branch is followed; if the condition is not met, the No-branch is followed.

Arrow: Indicates the flow of the events.

On the next page is a flow chart of a simple reaction time experiment with one practice block and one experimental block.

Note that if this way of visualising an experiment immediately strikes you as a great way to organise your thoughts into a workable design, then that is wonderful. However, if you feel it is a tedious amount of work that constrains your creativity by needlessly imposing order, then you might do best to save yourself the amount of paper involved. After all, some people prefer to work at a messy office desk. However, even if this is the case, we hope you will try to understand the endeavour as we will be illustrating various aspects of E-Prime® using these flowcharts.

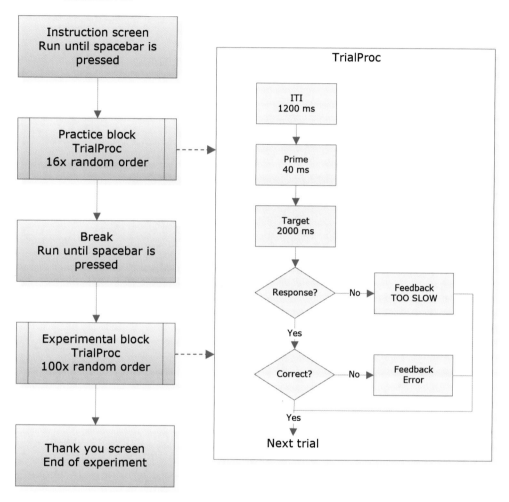

Now, let's get back to the more practical work and have a look at E-Studio!

E-Studio's structure

Here's an example of what an experiment looks like when we open it in E-Studio.

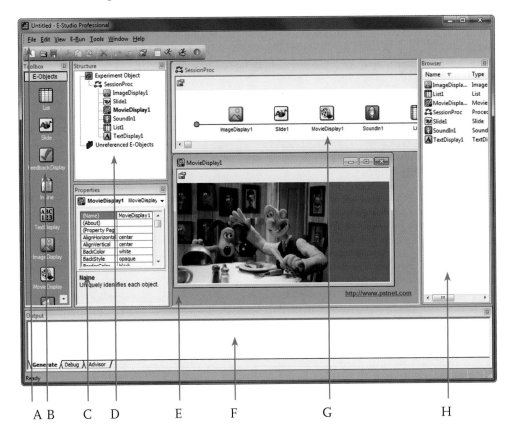

A B   C   D   E   F   G   H

A. In the **Menu** you can perform a number of typical Windows operations, such as opening and saving your experiment. In addition, by clicking on *View*, you can open the other areas (B – G and a few other ones). By clicking the *Run* icon – ⚒ – or pressing *F7*, you can compile and run the experiment. Use the E-Run Test icon 🔨 to run a quick test of your experiment (E-Prime 2 only; E-Prime 1 users may consider the **Clock.Scale** code described in Chapter IV).

▸ To abort an experiment early, press **control+alt+shift** to **terminate** the E-Run application.

B. The **Toolbox** area shows all components (E-Objects) available in E-Prime®. To use one of them, drag it onto either the Structure area (D) or a **Procedure object** (G). Here is a favourite trick: right-click on them, unselect *Large icons* and *voilà*: more screen *real estate*!

C. The **Properties window** displays the properties of the currently selected instance. By selecting the TextDisplay, for example (see below), one can quickly change certain properties (such as the background colour) from within the properties area. Typically, you can also use the working area (E) for that, by clicking on the hand (see right), which tends to be easier. 🖐

D. The **Structure window** shows the hierarchy of the experiment. Most experiments are organised into **blocks** and **trials**. For example, you may want an experiment to have two blocks: one for training your participants, followed by one for testing them.

E. This area – which covers almost half the screen – is called the **Workspace**. This is where you can edit elements of the experiment in a visual, easy way. When you double click on an object in the Structure window, it appears in the Working Area.

F. The **Output window** appears when you click the *Generate* button in order to compile the experiment. If there is an error in your experiment, the output window will show a message describing that error. In *E-Prime 2 Professional* an Experiment Advisor is available for detecting design and timing errors.

G. The **Procedure object** called **SessionProc** displays a timeline with the main Procedure of the experiment.

H. The **Browser window** shows all objects (instances) that you have created for the experiment. In the Browser window you can copy objects. E-Prime® then creates a new instance with the same properties as the original object. You can also copy objects by dragging the object with your mouse while holding down your *ctrl* key. If you simply want to reuse the same object at a different location of the experiment hold down *ctrl+shift* while dragging.

E-Objects

E-Prime® contains different objects, each with its own characteristic features and purposes. Here is an overview of the objects that are used most often.

 A **Procedure** is used to determine the order of events in an experiment.

 A **List** contains rows of items with specific properties (attributes).

 An **ImageDisplay** displays a picture.

 A **TextDisplay** displays one or more lines of text.

 A **MovieDisplay** displays a short movie clip.

 A **Slide** is a container type of object which can simultaneously present text, images, sound and so on.

 A **FeedbackDisplay** gives specific feedback on the participant's response to a stimulus.

 A **SoundIn** is used to record sounds.

 A **SoundOut** presents a sound file (.wav/.mp3/.wma).

 An **InLine** is used to add E-Basic script.

 A **Label** indicates a particular location on the timeline. The program can 'jump' backwards or forwards to a Label, in order to repeat or skip a part of the Procedure.

 A **PackageCall** contains reusable blocks of E-Basic script written by users of E-Prime 2 (often used in Procedures, which are used repeatedly or, for instance, in connecting equipment such as an eye-tracker to an E-Prime® experiment). As packages are beyond the scope of this book, please see the 'New Features Guide' for E-Prime 2 for a more detailed description.

Procedures, Lists and TextDisplays

A **Procedure** is the highest unit in the hierarchy of E-Prime®. It is used to specify the sequence of events in the experiment.

A Procedure is depicted as a timeline. The green ball on the left indicates the start of the Procedure and the red ball on the right depicts the end of the Procedure. In this example, the Procedure called 'TestProc' presents two TextDisplays. First, it shows the Wait1000ms TextDisplay, followed by the PressSpace TextDisplay.

When you open a new experiment, it already contains a Procedure, specifying the order of events in an experimental session. This Procedure is called 'SessionProc' by default.

Lists are extremely useful objects. They repeat and reorder Procedures. Consequently, they determine the way in which Procedures are repeated, for instance, randomising certain variables that are contained in the List.

When you create a new List, you will see this window:

The rows contain different items, the columns indicate the properties (called **attributes**) of these items.

By clicking on the *Add Level* icon or the *Add Multple Levels* icon , you can add one or more rows, respectively.

By clicking on the *Add Attribute* icon or the *Add Multiple Attributes* icon , you can add one or more columns, respectively.

Each list has a column named 'Procedure'. By filling in the name of a Procedure in a particular row, you specify which Procedure is used by that row. If the Procedure name doesn't yet exist in the experiment, the following pop-up window appears, telling you that the Procedure doesn't yet exist and asking you whether the Procedure should be created. Click *Yes*.

Subsequently, E-Prime® asks if this Procedure should be the default Procedure for newly created levels. Click *Yes* if you want all rows to use the same Procedure.

When you specify a Procedure, it will appear in the Structure window under the List containing the Procedure, as in the example (left), where *PracticeList* uses a Procedure called 'TrialProc'.

Lists are explained in more detail in Chapter II. For now, it will be enough that **Weight** indicates the number of repetitions of a particular item.

TextDisplays

TextDisplays present text in a singular formatting. This one shows the instruction to press the *space bar*. TextDisplays also offer a feature that may be even more important than showing text on the screen: they can collect responses. This, amongst others, is discussed in detail below.

The TextDisplay is the simplest way of showing stimuli and collecting responses and almost the only object required to make a simple Stroop experiment (see Chapter II). Later on, we will see that other objects, such as the Slide and the FeedbackDisplay, can *contain* TextDisplays.

When you drag a TextBox from the Toolbox area onto a Procedure and double click on it, you should see something like the screenshot, with the exception that it is usually named differently and doesn't say 'PRESS SPACE'.

The TextDisplay's name is shown at the top left corner. When you add a new TextDisplay to the experiment, it will be named 'TextDisplay1' (or 'TextDisplay2', if 'TextDisplay1' already exists). It is good practice to rename the objects and give  each of them a *unique and descriptive* name without funky characters such as commas, semicolons, spaces, etc. The above example admittedly shows how *not* to name an object: sensory presentations in experiments are stimuli by default, which makes this name not at all descriptive or unique.

Once you have created a TextDisplay, you can click on the *Properties* symbol to open the *Properties window*. This window has different tabs, allowing you to define various aspects of the object.

Common tab

Name: The tag you give the object, which provides a handle for calling its properties. Note that some names are prohibited since they would interfere with generating script: names like IF, THEN, TextDisplay, and so on, should be avoided, as well as spaces and special characters.

Tag: Insert here – although we generally omit this step – an identifier for your TextDisplay.

Notes: Here you can write a description of your TextDisplay. This can be very useful if, for instance, you want someone else to work on your experiment and quickly give them an idea about what the object does, and why. In theory, commenting code is extremely important, as it is very easy to forget what your code does. However, it is probably best to design your experiment in such a way that deep scrutiny on the contents of Notes is redundant.

Generate PreRun/PostRun: These properties affect the moment of the .Load method. If they are set to TopOfProcedure, this TextDisplay's properties will be loaded at the beginning of the Procedure. This can provide a timing benefit when the object is supposed to be shown by displacing the loading requirements in time to a period that is presumably 'non-time critical'. However, note that this is only convenient if the object properties are fully known at the beginning of such a Procedure. If this is not the case, it is best to set the PreRun/PostRun to before/after object run.

Handles Conditional Exit: If enabled (which it is by default), this should provide a method to gracefully exit E-Prime®. It is true that *control+alt+shift* immediately shuts down the currently running experiment, but the immediacy of it can also be problematic: it doesn't close devices and no edat file is generated (but see E-Recovery). E-Prime 2 (but only Professional) users can press **control+alt+backspace** during the experiment and gracefully terminate experiments.

General tab

Text: Here you should enter the text that the TextDisplay will show. Generally, you may find it easier to adjust the Text property by using the more graphical interface shown earlier (the figure showing the 'PRESS SPACE' TextDisplay), but it is important to remember that *.Text* is a property of a TextDisplay, which can be used when you start writing your own script in the later chapters.

AlignHorizontal, AlignVertical: Adjusting these properties adjusts the position of the text relative to the horizontal and vertical dimensions, respectively.

ForeColor: The colour of the text. You can choose a fixed colour name, e.g. *red*, *green*, or *black* from the dropdown menu. Alternatively, you can enter an RGB (Red, Green, Blue) value: three numbers ranging from 0 to 255, representing the relative amount of red, green and blue. Thus, (255,0,0) means red, (0,255,0) means green, (0,0,255) means blue, (255,255,255) means white, and (0,0,0) means black. In this way, you can easily 'mix' your own shades: (12,188,180) is turquoise, for example.

BackColor: The colour of the background. Specified in the same way as ForeColor.

BackStyle: The background colour may also be transparent; i.e. see-through. This is generally not very useful for TextDisplays, but for other objects, such as Slides, it might be practical.

ClearAfter: Specifies whether or not the screen is cleared after the presentation of TextDisplay. Usually, it doesn't matter what you specify here, because the Display is overwritten by the presentation of the next object anyway. It is also *deprecated*, according to Psychology Software Tools, by which software companies generally mean a function is still there to provide backward functionality, but should be avoided for it will be removed in a later version.

WordWrap: Specifies whether E-Prime® should automatically insert 'enters' when the text doesn't fit anymore. Without WordWrap on, E-Prime® will simply cut off the text where the screen ends.

Display Name: *E-Prime 2 Professional* adds the feature to use multiple displays independently. Here, you can select the display to use for this specific Stimulus.

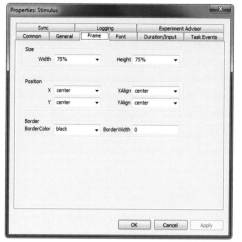

Frame tab

In the **Frame** tab, you can specify a rectangular area of the screen in which the object is presented. This area is called the 'Frame'.

Under **Size** you can specify the **Width** and **Height** of the frame. You can either specify the size relatively (in percentage of the total screen size) or absolutely (in pixels). Note that this is 75% by default as in the *Production Release* version of E-Prime® (2.0.10.242).

If the Frame is smaller than the screen, you can specify its position on the screen under **Position**. You can set four different parameters. **XAlign** and **YAlign** specify which point of the frame is used as a reference for placing the frame on the screen. **X** and **Y** specify the horizontal and vertical position of the frame's reference point on the screen. You can compare it to putting a piece of paper on a pinboard. The parameters **XAlign** and **YAlign** specify the position of the pin relative to the paper, the parameters **X** and **Y** specify the position of the pin on the pinboard (see examples below).

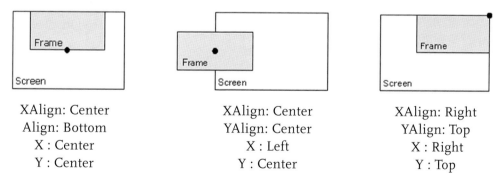

XAlign: Center	XAlign: Center	XAlign: Right
Align: Bottom	YAlign: Center	YAlign: Top
X : Center	X : Left	X : Right
Y : Center	Y : Center	Y : Top

BorderColor: Shows the color of the border, if BorderWidth is greater than 0.

BorderWidth: With this property, you can set the width of the border around the TextDisplay in number of pixels.

Font tab

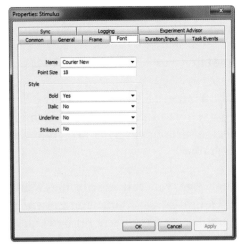

Name: The type of font to use in this TextDisplay.

Point Size: The size of the font in points. This is the standard unit of font that is used in all Windows applications, but be careful: most experiments run in a lower resolution than normal, so fonts tend to look bigger when running the experiment.

Bold: Shows the word in a thicker typeface, which is pretty self-evident, but please note that E-Prime's default for Bold is *on*.

Duration tab

This is probably the single-most important tab. Here, you adjust the timing part of the stimulus, stimulus duration adjustments being crucial (some might say: tantamount) to classic cognitive experiments. In addition, it is where you select which input devices (such as keyboard, mouse, Serial Response Box) are used to record responses. The tab also deals with most other aspects of responding: 'what should happen after a response?', 'what was the correct answer?', etc.

Duration: With this property, you can manipulate how long the TextDisplay is presented on the screen. When you set this to -1, it acts the same as when you select the infinite duration.

Timing Mode: E-Prime® is praised for its timing accuracy and its developers claim that E-Prime® can have sub-millisecond accuracy (i.e. have random timing errors with a standard deviation of less than one millisecond). However, this all depends on which other processes are running in the background, which hardware is installed, and whether unrelated software like Norton Antivirus is allowed to run alongside E-Prime®.

More on timing issues later, but for now, here is the basic story. It takes time (mere milliseconds, or even less) between the moment when E-Prime's clock notices that an event should be triggered and when that object is actually presented. Because of this, events may not synchronise with time, which E-Prime® calls 'cumulative drift'. To prevent this, you can change the TimingMode to Cumulative, which changes the duration of this TextDisplay to adjust for this drift. Which TimingMode you should use depends on your experiment. If your experiment consists of relatively long inter-stimulus intervals (say, a few seconds) and timing is not crucial, using the Event Mode may suffice. However, if your experiment depends critically on timing, such as when presenting subliminal stimuli with a duration of 20 ms, you may need to use the Cumulative Mode. However, Procedures using objects in this mode can behave oddly and unpredictably, especially when they include *Terminate* End actions (see description below) or scripts. When timing is critical, you should refer to the chapter on 'Critical Timing' in the 'User's Guide'.

The other way to cope with a certain type of timing error is the **PreRelease**. Suppose you wish to present high-resolution images, perhaps even in a rapid serial visual presentation task. In this case, E-Prime® will have a hard time loading all those large image files. In order to alleviate the stress E-Prime® puts on your processor, you can use TextDisplays prior to the pictures you want to use and set some PreRelease to that TextDisplay. This PreRelease time is used to load the oncoming picture, sound or other 'heavy' object into memory while the current TextDisplay is still shown. Then, when it is show-time, E-Prime® has already loaded the object, thereby decreasing onset errors in the next stimulus. If timing is critical in your experiment, we recommended that you study the 'Critical Timing' chapter in the E-Prime® 'User's Guide'.

⫸ Notice that, following the *Production Release* of E-Prime 2, the PreRelease is always set to: *(Same as duration)*. While this will make it much less likely that your experiment will have timing problems, the degree to which subsequent objects will be run *before* the PreReleasing object ends can make your life difficult. In particular, care should be taken when 1) the next object on the timeline is an InLine or a PackageCall; 2) the object with PreRelease is the last object on the timeline; or, 3) the next object is a FeedbackDisplay.

The **Data Logging** property has a few options allowing you to log various timing and response parts of the TextDisplay. We would suggest leaving this untouched and selecting the logging properties in the *Logging tab*, as E-Prime® generally logs far too much if you allow it to. However, we once observed the reaction of someone who had logged everything BUT the critical response times and came up with a convenient rule of thumb: it is better to log too much than too little.

If you want the participant to respond to the TextDisplay, you will have to add an **InputDevice**. To do so, click on *Add* and select *Keyboard* or *Mouse*. More devices (such as the Serial Response Box) can be available, but you will need to add them first by clicking on *Edit > Experiment > Devices > Add*.

After an InputDevice is selected, you can edit which keys are **Allowable**. Normally, you enter a range of characters here, for example: Allowable: abcd. Then, all four keys (a, b, c, d) are seen as valid responses. Pressing *e* or *A* (*shift+a*), for example, will not do anything. If you want to use the space bar or other special keys, you will have to use the round brackets and *capitalised* letters: *Allowable: {SPACE}* for example. The default ({ANY}) is not recommended for a serious experiment, since accidental key-presses should not be counted as 'real' responses.

Whereas the Allowable part generally has several options, usually only one of them is **Correct**. It is important to understand the *fundamental difference* between the allowable and the correct response. As a rule of thumb, then: the allowable set of responses covers the range of possible responses and *is generally the same for each trial*; the correct response is typically only the one response that the participant *should* have made and *is generally different for each trial* (although one can, in E-Prime 2 Professional, have multiple correct responses). It is probably best to think of 'correct response' in terms of accuracy, rather than appropriateness. Both in the case of {ANY} response being allowable, and if only one key is allowed, the accuracy of the response becomes pretty meaningless.

The correct response doesn't have to be specified. For example, a welcome screen doesn't have a correct response. It can simply be closed after pressing a specific key. On the other hand, the allowable response should always be specified. If you have failed to do so, and the duration is set to infinite, your experiment will get stuck, since the participant can't press any key to close the TextDisplay.

By adjusting the **Time Limit** property, you can increase or decrease the amount of time, following the onset of the stimulus, in which a response is logged. Often, this will be the same as the **Duration** of the stimulus, which is the selected option by default. That way, if the duration of a stimulus is 2000 ms, a response will still be logged when it follows 1999 ms after the onset of the stimulus. However, it is possible to ignore extremely late responses (outliers), by setting the Time Limit to 1000 ms. A response that follows 1100 ms after the onset will then not be logged. It is also possible to log responses even longer than the duration of the stimulus. If, for example, you use a subliminal priming paradigm, you could set the Duration of the stimulus at 20 ms, but the Time Limit at 1000 ms. Then, responses are logged relative to the onset of the subliminal stimulus, even if it is no longer being shown.

End Action specifies which action to undertake when the participant responds. By setting this to *Terminate* (default), for example, the TextDisplay is immediately wiped off the screen when an allowable response is given. The **Jump** option will be discussed in a later chapter.

Sync tab

The Sync tab enables you to switch on on- and offset synchronisation. To understand what synchronisation is about, you must grasp a basic fact about both

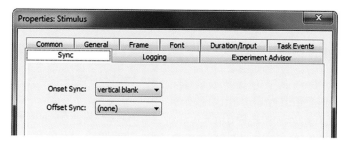

cathode ray tube (CRT – or, the 'old' type) and *liquid crystal display* (LCD – or, the 'flat' type) computer monitors: each dot (pixel) you see on the screen is updated sequentially: that is, from up to down. Although it may look as if the pixels you see on the screen are static (especially with LCD monitors), in fact they are updated at a rate of at least 60 times each second: 60 Hz (or about 100 Hz when using ancient CRT monitors, which are actually better for doing experiments). Crucially for psychologists, especially those working with perception and (sub-liminal) priming, the presentation of visual stimuli is constrained by the timing characteristics of the monitor.

Consider, for example, a psychologist who wants to show a subliminal prime, say, a smiling face, 10 milliseconds before the onset of a word to which the participant is required to react. When **Onset Sync** and **Offset Sync** are turned off, and the experiment is running on a 60 Hz monitor (still a standard especially in LCD), the screen is updated every (1000 / 60 =) 17 ms. When E-Prime® is programmed to show the smiley, it sends 'commands to the screen', but there is no way to know exactly how and what it shows: it may show everything 17 ms later, for 17 ms, because it just finished updating the screen; but it may also show only half a smiley because the updating cycle just got round to half the screen on its up to down route. This phenomenon is called **screen tearing**. The same may then happen with the word to be responded to. However, if we enable Onset Sync for both the prime and the word, E-Prime® will wait until the screen is able to show the word fully. The only problem then is that it must show the prime for at least as long as the refresh cycle (17 ms) lasts, thus creating a timing error here of 7 ms as it is impossible to show anything for less than 17 ms.

For exactly this reason, we recommend the use of (often ridiculously old) monitors that have shorter refresh cycles (100 Hz – 10 ms; which gives nice, round numbers), so we can safely use Onset Sync by default. However, obtaining these monitors is becoming increasingly difficult, *sic transit gloria mundi*.

Note that the Onset Sync is set to *vertical blank* by default. This helps avoid screen tearing, an issue we will explain later when discussing display hardware.

Logging tab

If, like us, you love reaction times and other chronometric measures, E-Prime® is the thing for you. Not only does it let you collect standard outcome measures, such as response, accuracy and reaction time, but it also provides an arsenal of auditing weaponry to bedazzle even the most number-crazed statisticians. For example, if you wish to check whether E-Prime® *really* presents your stimuli for *t* milliseconds, you can **log** the duration error.

You can select as many values to log as you like, but try to be somewhat pragmatic: you may want to log the time it took for a participant to read the introduction-screen, so you can log RT for this display. On the other hand, we have yet to hear from a psychologist who is interested in the timing accuracy of this introduction-screen, so you don't generally log OnsetDelay, for instance.

Often, a psychological experiment requires only one response for each single trial. For example, in a Stroop task, each displayed word requires one reaction. This translates, *e-wise*, in that the text display, which displays the word 'WHITE', collects responses (such as the correct answer: black). For this object, favourite logging properties would then be:

- **CRESP**: Correct response. As stated above, typically depends on the condition and trial.
- **RESP**: The actual response.
- **ACC**: The accuracy, defined as 1 if the RESP and CRESP are equal and otherwise 0.
- **RT**: Reaction, or response time (ms), which is RTTime − OnsetTime.
- **OnsetDelay**: Difference between programmed time the stimulus was to be presented (in the case of visual stimuli: on the screen) and the actual time its presentation started.
- **DurationError**: Difference between the prescribed duration the stimulus was to be shown on screen and the actual time. Or strictly speaking: OffsetTime + PreRelease − OnsetTime − Duration.

Which logging properties you should use, depends on your experiment. Three other valuable logging properties are:

- **RTTime**: Time stamp of the reaction relative to the beginnig of the experiment (ms).
- **OnsetTime**: Time stamp of stimulus onset relative to the beginning of the experiment (ms).
- **OffsetTime**: Time stamp of the end of the presentation of the stimulus (ms) relative to the beginning of the experiment. Notice, however, that this is not necessarily when the stimulus ends: a visual stimulus remains 'on the screen' as long as no other stimulus overwrites it, and an audio file of 4 seconds long may contain 2 seconds of silence.

Tutorial I: A simple RT experiment

Do you, like Michiel's cat (right), have 'lightning reflexes'? Believe it or not, many first-time participants who are unfamiliar with psychological experiments want to know 'how well they did' and considering that your first priority is most likely not pinning someone on a kind of normal (vs abnormal!) distribution, it is always good to tell them they were *'quite fast...'*. Let's find out how to do this!

It can be hard to start programming an experiment from scratch, so you may find it easier to follow a certain process schema. First, and crucially, what is it that you want your participants to see during an experiment – what do you know from your own experiences with psychological research in the lab? Imagine *examples*, rather than defining everything beforehand: instead of trying, for example, to show Stroop-like stimuli, ask yourself: 'so what is a Stroop-like stimulus?' 'Well', you answer, 'something like the word *red* written in *blue*'. Then, define the Procedure of a trial as the sequential presentation of such stimuli.

Common elements of an experiment include:

Trials: Typically, this includes:

- A fixation: This stimulus that is often shaped like a crosshair or addition sign 'warns' the participant that the interesting stimulus is approaching.
- The target: The interesting stimulus itself, to which the participant is to respond.
- Some form of feedback (occasionally).

Blocks: Are defined by the number and variant of trials they contain. For instance,

- A training block may contain some 20 trials and is used to get the participant accustomed to the experiment.
- A testing block contains more trials, depending on the variability of the outcome measures, the number of conditions, etc.

Step 1: Building the basic hierarchy

- Open E-Studio, select *Blank experiment.*

- Save your experiment in a location where you can find it again easily (e.g. a USB stick, your personal drive, etc.). Give the experiment a unique name that doesn't contain weird characters (slashes, dots, etc.).

- Make sure you always save your work. Keep your file structure well-organised! Subsequent chapters may ask you to re-use part of your earlier work. There is an additional advantage: by saving your work you also start a personal collection of experiments that may serve as a source for future reference.

- In the Structure view, double-click on *SessionProc* ; you will see a timeline popping up:

- Drag a List from the Toolbox to the SessionProc to the timeline and call it 'BlockList' (this is a conventional name; you can also use any other name as long as it doesn't contain strange characters or spaces).

- Double-click on the *BlockList* and add one row by clicking on the icon of the arrow pointing down.

- Change the name of the Procedure column of the first row to 'TrainingProc' by editing the text. Please note that it is also possible to click on the down triangle next to the name and change the Procedure to an existing one: SessionProc. *DO NOT DO THIS!* For some reason, this seems the most intuitive action and we have seen many students astonished at how fatally E-Prime® crashes when this seemingly minor mistake is made.

- E-Prime® will ask you whether you really want to create this new Procedure – TrainingProc – and here you select *Yes.* If E-Prime® asks you whether you want this Procedure to be the default one, select *No.*

- Change the name of the *Procedure* column of the second row to 'TestingProc' and repeat the previous actions (*Yes, No*). Notice that *not* creating the new procedure will result in a bug.

- Double-click on the *TrainingProc* and add a List there. Rename (select and press *F2*) the List as TrainingList. Double-click on the *TestingProc* and add a List there, rename it as TestingList.

- Edit *TrainingList* and make the weight of the first and only row 10. In the Procedure column, write down the name 'TrialProc'.

- Edit *TestingList* and make the weight of the first and only row 20, then write down the name 'TrialProc' as its Procedure.

- Now you have the basic hierarchy of an experiment: one experiment with two blocks, one for training and one for testing, and the two blocks run the same Procedure; the training 10 times, the testing 20. You can check whether you successfully completed this step by matching your screen with the screenshot below.

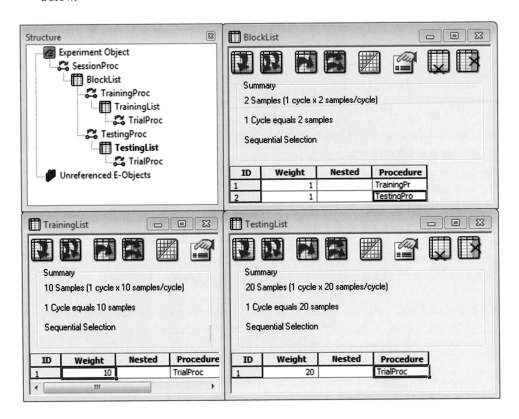

You could also consider dropping the *BlockList* and simply running the *TrainingList* and *TestingList* consecutively in your *SessionProc*. However, we think that the BlockList solution has many advantages. For example, while testing whether your experiment runs correctly, you can easily skip parts of it by setting the weights of the respective rows to 0. Moreover, if you want to abort your experiment with *Inline scripts*, you can do so by simply terminating the BlockList (see Chapter V). The BlockList is also a proper place to nest Lists used for counterbalance/between-subject manipulation purposes (see Chapter III). The attributes of these *nested Lists* are then automatically inherited by Lists lower in the experimental hierarchy.

Step 2: Programming the trial

- The trial is perhaps the most important unit in your programming experiments. Here, you will be showing your participant a fixation for 500 ms, and a target for an infinite – or until key-press – amount of time.

- Double-click on the *TrialProc* and drag two TextDisplays to the timeline. Name the first 'Fixation' and the second 'TargetStimulus'.

- Edit the Fixation to show a single '+' sign and to have a duration of 500 ms. This is our 'inter-trial interval' (ITI).

- Edit the TargetStimulus to show the command 'Press space!' and to have an infinite duration. Then, add an input-device by clicking on *Add* in the *Duration/Input tab*, and choose *keyboard*. Set, as the only *Allowable* key, {SPACE}. Mind the capitals, they are important here. Also, set the spacebar as the only *correct* key (this is generally not the case!) and accept the standard type of logging.

- Your experiment should run now, so try this. It is good practice to run your experiment *frequently*, because this makes it easier for you to diagnose, or **debug**, problems. Run your experiment with any subject number but 0, or else nothing is logged. Remember: if you want to abort the experiment quickly, you can always press *control+alt+shift* (or perhaps *control+shift+backspace*). When starting your experiment, the resolution of your screen may change. In Chapter III we will discuss how to change these screen settings.

Step 3: Analyse the data

- When you have finished testing the experiment, start *E-DataAid* and open the data you generated. These can be found in the same folder where your experiment was last saved.

- Scroll through your data and note the various columns. For example, notice how the trial number starts at 1 and goes on to 10, because the first block (the TrainingList) is finished after 10 trials; then starts at 1 again but now goes to 20, because the second block (the TestingList) is finished after 20 trials.

- Since we want to know what your participant's average basic reaction time was, the TargetStimulus.RT is most important to us. Notice how several values will be well below (approaching an unlikely 0) and above (in case you were distracted) the average. Apparently, a bit of filtering needs to happen to get a clear picture of your RT in comparison to your neighbour's.

- Click on *Tools*, select *Analyze* and click on *Filter*. In the dropdown box, select *TargetStimulus.RT* (in alphabetical order here) and click on *Checklist*. Now, click once on the first value that is higher or equal to 100, then scroll down, and *shift+click* on the last value that is lower than 1000. Only then, with all the values you want to include selected, press *spacebar* and click on *OK*. In this way you prevent outlying RT values from distorting your mean RT values.

> ⫸ Consider what would happen if you save this analysis and apply it to another dataset later. In this case, it is quite likely that there are new unique RT values in your dataset not yet included in your checklist. In other words, you have to reselect the relevant RTs. In those cases it might be preferable to use the Range alternative. Click *Range...* and set the first range to *Greater than or equal* 100, combined with the second range being *Less than* 1000. Don't forget to select the *AND* operator, since our inclusion criterion is that each single RT needs to meet both conditions.

- So now that we have deleted the outliers from further analysis, close the filter and drag TargetStimulus.RT from the list of variables to *Data*. Click on *Run* and get ready to be astounded by your reaction time! Michiel's was 191 ms.

One of the reasons why many people use E-DataAid in conjunction with E-Prime® is the ease with which you can make crosstabs. Here is how we do it:

- Close the analysis results and, without changing anything else, drag the Procedure[Block] variable from the list to either the row or the columns (try both). Again, click on *Run*.

This is what it should look like:

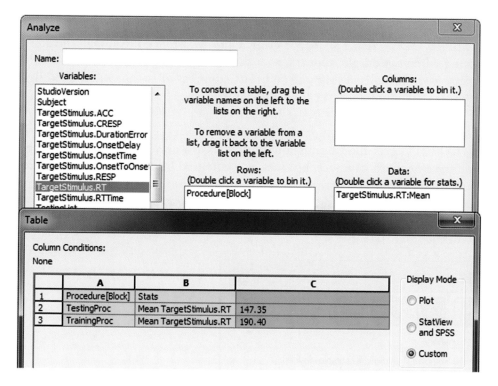

- So, Michiel was about 43 ms faster after training a bit.

Exercises

- Add an introduction screen to the start of your experiment, with infinite duration, terminating when the participant presses a certain unique key ('press C to continue').

- Add a goodbye screen and a thank you screen to your experiment.

- Use the mouse instead of the keyboard as InputDevice for the TargetStimulus. To do this, you basically do the same as you did with the keyboard as an input device, except that the response keys are defined as 1 (left mouse-button) and

2 (right mouse-button). Therefore, if you enter '12' as allowable both buttons are allowable responses.

- Pimp your experiment: adjust it to your taste or to what you think would be wise; just experiment with all the options.

- Design an experiment to test the following hypothesis: it is easier to respond to green than to red. The idea is clear: typically, we need to stop doing something when a red light appears, so a psychologist could hypothesise that because we internalised this rule and thus suppress all action when a red light appears. It is time to find out whether this is true.

You can base this experiment on the one you made in the tutorial. First, the trial needs to be changed: the fixation should now have a gray background; the target should have no word anymore, but just be a coloured background. The Training-List should now have *white* targets. The TestingList should now have *green* and *red* targets. Therefore, the TestingList should get one extra row, so that there are two different procedures. Instead of having the TestingList call "TrialProc", let it refer to "RedProc" and "GreenProc":

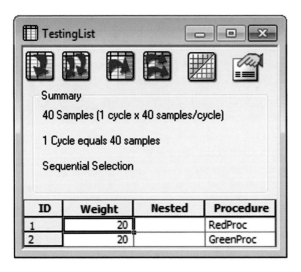

ID	Weight	Nested	Procedure
1	20		RedProc
2	20		GreenProc

⟶ At this point, you might think: would it not be much easier to *reuse* the same Procedure but only change one aspect – or variable – of the trial? In the next chapter, you will find out that this is indeed the case and you will learn how to do this using *attributes*.

Also, randomise the selection between these two Procedures (see the List properties) so that the participant can't know in advance what colour the target will be. Edit both the RedProc and GreenProc equally so that they are exactly the same in terms of look, duration and response, except that the background of the target differs.

Test your experiment: is it easier to respond to green than to red?

Advanced Exercises

- Instead of analysing all data separately for each participant or cutting and pasting data into Excel from various edat (.edat/.edat2) files, one can simply use E-Merge to merge edat datafiles together into one big file.

- Make sure you have more than one edat datafile (run your experiment with different subject numbers) and put them in a directory. Start E-Merge, go to the directory containing the files using the folder tree and first filter that directory so you can only see the edat files and not anything else (press the *Filter* button) and use *.edat or *.edat2 (the * wildcard means everything).

- Select the *.edat* or *.edat2* files and press the *Merge* button (use the standard merge). Now you will see that an .emrg or .emrg2 file has been created containing all the information from the two separate files.

- Now use E-DataAid to analyse all your participants/sessions at once.

Chapter II

Attributes, Slides and more on Lists

In this chapter, you will learn

About: • Experimental design in E-Prime®
        • Latent and manifest variables
        • More on Lists
        • Attributes everywhere
        • Images
        • Slides and feedback

How to: • Program basic conflict experiments (Stroop, Simon)
        • Program Implicit Association Task

In the previous chapter, you have learned how to present texts, using TextDisplays. In this chapter, you will learn how to use ImageDisplays to present images, Slides to present combinations of images and texts, and FeedbackDisplays to present feedback about the participant's performance. Most experiments consist of multiple trials that are similar in some respects, but different in others (e.g. they display different words, numbers, images, colours or shapes). Rather than having to program each trial separately, you can use Lists that contain your trials. The List specifies which properties (attributes) of the trials are fixed and which vary from trial to trial. The List also specifies how often each trial is repeated and in which order the trials are presented to different participants (for example, fixed or random).

After completing this chapter, you will be able to program experiments such as the famous Stroop task and Simon task. Moreover, you will be able to discover the hidden stereotypical thoughts of your friends, by having them perform the Implicit Association Task that you will create in Tutorial III.

Experimental design in E-Prime®

When it comes to programming experiments in E-Prime®, it is crucial to define every part of your design to the fullest extent. This is true for psychological reasons – you will want to know beforehand how long you want to display 'Drink Coca-Cola' in order for your prime to be subliminal; whether *teal* and *terracotta* are proper Stroop words, and so on. But this is obvious. However, the baffling complexity of modern computers easily hides their simple natures: they are *not aware of your grand designs*.

One of the first ways to approach programming software is to start with a good plan. For example, John Ridley Stroop may have said to himself, back in 1935: 'Reading may be an automatic process that can interfere, or inhibit, other skills, such as naming colours'. To test it, he had to go one step further: 'If reading and naming interfere with one another, then [...] naming the colour in which a word was printed should be slower if the colour of the ink is incompatible with the word that was printed (e.g. 'blue' vs. 'blue')'. If he would have had access to, but not quite the experience in, E-Prime®, he would ask E-Prime® to 'print words and colours in compatible colours', but E-Prime® would not know *what* words, *which* colours and *what compatibility* means. Our favourite way to approach definitions is to just name *all possible combinations*. It takes a bit of time, but it is foolproof.

So, staying with Stroop, let's say we have two colours, red and green, and two words, 'red' and 'green'. This would give us the following four combinations:

Colour	Word
Red	Red
Red	Green
Green	Red
Green	Green

This is the *online* bit E-Prime® cares about; they are what we call **manifest** or, if you prefer, explicit variables, as these are the ones that literally *explicate* the design as it *manifests* itself. They are quite unlike **latent** or implicit variables, in that these are generally the ones psychologists are most interested in: except to filter out the incidental colour-blind participant, Stroop was not concerned about colours and words as such, but their interference. So, to analyse the data, he might have added another variable to these two: *compatibility*. That way, he could average data from the compatible and incompatible conditions and measure the more general difference between the two.

Colour	Word	Congruence
Red	Red	Congruent
Red	Green	Incongruent
Green	Red	Incongruent
Green	Green	Congruent

In other words: start with writing out all combinations ('cells') of manifest variables – the number of cells should always equal the product of the number of categories within each variable – then add latent variables for your own convenience. But: having different variables – even if they are manifest – doesn't automatically entail that E-Prime® will *do* anything with them; for that, we need Lists.

More on lists

With Lists, we can control the sequence and selection of experimental (manifest) variables. A variable, as entered in a List in E-Prime®, is called an **attribute**, and is generally anchored to the current context of the List. Consider the previous List of four different types of Stroop stimuli (based on the colour – red or green – and the word – red or green). Especially when you have made a little, digital sketch of your design by writing down all different combinations of categories, you can easily copy-paste the values from Excel or Word to an E-Prime® List:

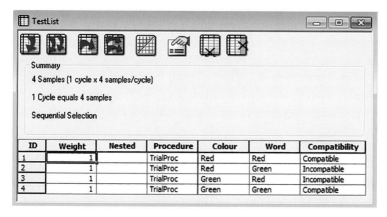

Notice the ID tag of each row here. When going through a List, and it is randomised, all E-Prime® really does is randomise the ID tags, such that their order becomes 2413 instead of 1234, for instance. In this particular scenario, the first trial will call the context of ID 2 (with a red colour and green word), followed by ID 4 (with a green colour and red word), and so on. If, instead of using weights, you edit the number of **cycles** (see below), this order is randomised after each time a List is finished running (in this case, after four trials). Later chapters will clarify what this means when you are dealing with 'scripting'. For now it is enough that you understand how Lists enable easy randomisation of your experimental conditions.

To change the order of a List from sequential to randomised, you will have to edit the properties of the List: 🖼. Some of the properties are best looked up in the E-Prime® 'User's Guide', as there are only a few rare cases where these come in handy, but please note the following more interesting properties:

Selection tab

Most important of all is the Order property. This is *sequential* (from the first to the last ID) by default. However, when presenting a trial list, you would probably choose a *random* order, which randomises the order of the IDs every time a **cycle** (defined by the number of **samples** and weights) has finished. If you choose *random with replacement*, the IDs are randomised at every sample: thus, a random (weighted by the number in the weight column) ID is picked every new trial. This will upset the balance of your trial list, since repetitions of combinations are very likely to occur (in this case the sequence of IDs 2222 is as likely to occur as 2413!), so it is generally *not* a good idea to carelessly pick random with replacement if you are not sure (but see also Blais [2008]).

Other, less typical forms of randomisation are *offset, counterbalance* and *permutation*. These have in common that the order is not exactly randomised, but balanced such that participants each get, for example, a random selection of IDs, yet in such a way that the orders themselves occur an equal number of times amongst participants (for example, participant 1 gets order 1234, participant 2 gets 2341, etc.). This is useful if you don't want to control something directly, but do want groups of equal size.

In many psychology experiments, it is useful to balance between stimulus-response mappings. This is called 'counterbalancing'. For example: half of the participants are required to respond left whenever they see a circle, the other half are required to respond right when they see a circle. By doing this, the combination of left-circle occurs equally often as the combination right-circle. Therefore, if some benefit for one of those combinations existed (very unlikely in this case), counterbalancing the stimulus-response mappings would correct this. If you need to balance instead of randomise sequences between or within subjects, use one of the following three methods:

Offset: Is almost exactly like a sequential order, except that the starting ID is defined by the subject's (or group or session) number. If you compare balancing to shuffling a deck of four cards: with each subject (or group or session), the top-most card is placed on the bottom. This essentially makes the order 1234 for the first participant, 2341 for the second, and 3412 for the 2003rd.

Counterbalance: Picks *one* ID from the List depending on the subject (or group or session) number, and uses this ID for the complete experimental session. As we will learn in Chapter III, this option is also very useful for between-subject designs.

Permutation: From amongst all possible permutations of the conditions, one arrangement is selected (or, likely, the nth permutation of conditions that can exist is generated). So, if you run blocks a, b and c (stored in ID 1, 2 and 3) in permutated arrangements, subject (or group or session) 1 gets order abc, subject 2 gets order acb, subject 6 gets order cba, subject 7 gets order abc, and so on.

Reset / Exit tab

This tab defines the sampling. As said, a List is randomised again if it has more than one cycle and one of the cycles has ended. A cycle then, is composed of a number of samples, either *All samples* (the sum of the weighted rows in the List) or *X samples*, in which X denotes the number of samples that are picked from the (weighted) List.

In most experimental designs, all aspects of the stimuli are *orthogonal*: the proportions of every experimental or non-experimental condition are kept equal. This ensures that every participant encounters every combination of conditions the same number of times, which (partiallly) rules out strategy-based hypotheses. For example, if a psychologist interested in doing a Stroop experiment (and who would not be?) wants to find out whether the effect changes if the colour is shown 1000, 500 or 0 ms *before* the onset of the word, and uses a List of two words and two colours, the design should contain 3 x 2 x 2 = 12 rows.

By default, a cycle in E-Prime® has all of these 12 samples, so this researcher would choose *Random order* in the *Selection* tab, leave the *Reset sampling* to *All* (12) samples and make sure the List is 'recycled' a number of times.

How many cycles? The answer to this question is based on your continuing experience with behavioural experimental paradigms, but a few considerations are general:

- If you don't know, *pilot test* it yourself. Or better: annoy your friends by asking them, and they can also tell you whether your introduction is clear.

- Basically, you want to end up with enough data for each participant that the variability in the outcome measures (e.g. reaction time) is smaller than the size of the effect. You can delete the inaccurate and outlying responses, so you will probably end up with fewer usable data than you might expect. So, more repetitions are useful. However, you don't want to torment your participant any longer than necessary, so enough is enough.

- How many cycles you need depends on your experiment. For some experiments ten repetitions of each trial might be enough, but for other experiments you might need as many as 30 to 50 repetitions.

⫸ Michiel is convinced that a typical behavioural experiment requires an average of 12 good repetitions for each cell in the final analysis over the latent variables and has been known to consider this the Magic Number 12. Given that we know that a normal participant is likely to sometimes press the wrong button, or forget to press any button on time, you will likely have to filter out some responses before your final analysis. So, if you expect (and you should do a pilot to find out) your participant to do this in about 20% of the time, having 15 repetitions is a good idea. Our Stroop experiment, with three offsets and two types of compatiblity should then have 6 x 15 = 90 trials. This is, of course, a minimum and a rule of thumb at that, so to get a nicely balanced design, you might consider 8 cycles (i.e. 8 x 12 = 96 trials) in all. Of course, many paradigms, in particular those involving psychophysiological apparatuses, require more trials.

Attributes

So, you have a List, your design is flawless, but still nothing changes when you run your experiment: your colours and words still do not show. To bring about your exciting, experimental manipulations, we need attributes: each and every property in your trial (or any other object that is of a lower level than the List) can make use of them. To do this, to manipulate a (manifest) variable by the List, so to speak, you merely have to fill in the name of that attribute, but with square brackets around it. Take our Stroop example, we can fill in the Word attribute instead of explicitly naming the word:

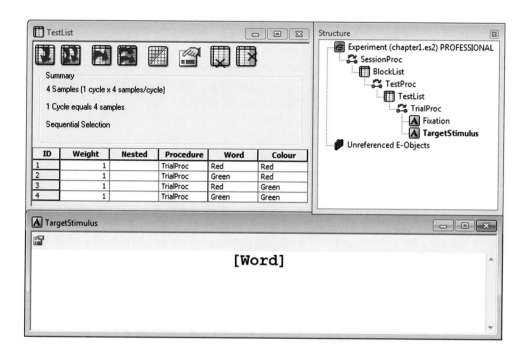

Now, instead of writing down the word for every new trial, E-Prime® does it for you. In trial 1 and 2, the participant will see (bearing in mind this List is not randomised) the word 'red'. In trial 3 and 4, the participant will see the word 'green'. Still, this is not quite a Stroop stimulus: every word is printed in black. However, as you may remember from Chapter I, the colour of the text can be changed by editing the ForeColour property of the TextDisplay. To manipulate it by referring to the List, you can just enter [Colour] in the *ForeColor* property. So, now we are finished with the perception aspect of the Stroop task: the first trial will show the word **red** in a red colour, the second the word **red** in a green colour.

However, in our experiment, which is based on the previous chapter's exercise, the participant doesn't really have to watch, he or she may just click on the right mouse-button every time any word is shown. To make a pure Stroop experiment, you should record the participant's voice as he or she mentions the name of the colour in which the word is printed. Alternatively, you could ask participants to respond by pressing a key on the keyboard; for example, 'r' for the word **red** or **green** printed in red, 'g' for the word **red** or **green** printed in green.

To do this:

- Add an attribute to the List called 'CorrectResponse', or something similar.

- Fill in the correct response for each row. In our List, we would add 'r' in the first row, 'g' in the second, and so on.

- Now check the properties of the Stroop stimulus and change the *correct* property (Duration / input tab) to refer to '[CorrectResponse]'.

Always remember that allowable refers to the *set* of allowed responses, not to any one particular response. Thus, in our case, with only 'r' and 'g' responses possible, it should say 'rg' (mind the lower case, otherwise your responses would only be captured if the *Caps Lock* were on!).

This is what it should look like:

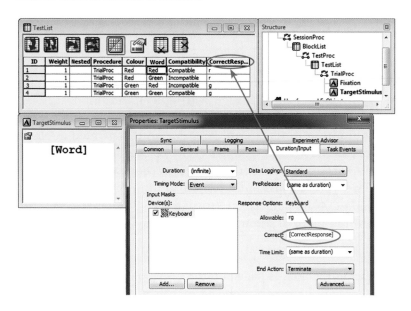

Another example of using attributes in E-Prime® will be covered in the Tutorial, but first: you may have wondered if editing text is the only thing you can do with E-Prime®. No, dear students, it is quite easy to add images, sound (Chapter III) and even video (with E-Prime 2), and it doesn't require much extra explanation, so let's see how images work.

Showing an image

You can show pictures by moving an **ImageDisplay** onto a Procedure, in the same way as you inserted a TextDisplay. The properties of ImageDisplays are almost exactly the same as those of TextDisplays:

The **Filename property** should mention the name of the picture you want to present. In the previous version of E-Prime® (E-Prime 1) this file had to be a BMP, a usually uncompressed, raster graphics image file format. However, in the current version of E-Prime® (E-Prime 2) images can also have the following formats: JPG, JPEG, GIF, PNG, TIF, TIFF, EMF, WMF. Most students are most familiar with JPEG and GIF formats, since these are most commonly found on the internet. However, it is bad practice to use these compressed images, since they lose part of the details in colour or pixels. Instead, we always ask our own students to try to use *MSPaint*, because 1) it ships with Windows (in *Accessories > Paint*); 2) it allows you to see the minute details by zooming in to 800%, after which editing single pixels becomes much easier; and 3) it allows conversion to **bitmap** (by saving as .bmp). Editing single pixels and paying an extraordinary amount of attention to your visual presentation are important skills if you want to work with images. For example: if you use multiple cards like the one above, make sure *all* are of equal width and height, say 100 x 200 pixels, because if you have one card that is 101 x 199 pixels, it will be distorted and thus immediately capture the participant's attention.

The **Mirror properties** flip the image horizontally (left / right) or vertically (up / down). This adjustment doesn't alter the quality of the images, unlike the following property.

By **stretching** you can adjust the image to the size of the frame (in % or pixels, see TextDisplay properties in Chapter I). Although this doesn't immediately show on screen, you can see the effect of this when you run the experiment. The example shows what to expect under different frame widths and heights and with stretching on and off.

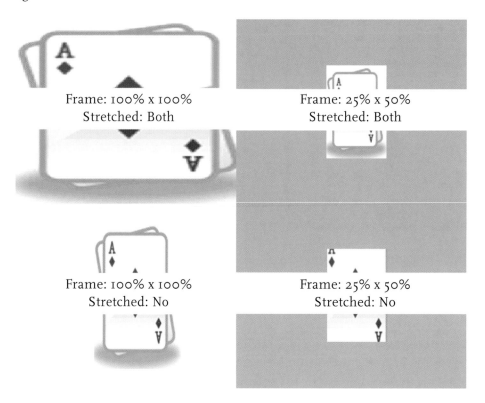

Frame: 100% x 100%
Stretched: Both

Frame: 25% x 50%
Stretched: Both

Frame: 100% x 100%
Stretched: No

Frame: 25% x 50%
Stretched: No

Please note that stretching generally leads to a noticeable loss in quality: if a picture of 100 x 100 pixels is stretched to accommodate a 150 x 150 frame, the computer can't modify the *pixel-size* directly, since this depends on the screen itself. Instead, half of the pixels will become twice as large; the other half will remain the same, causing your image to look messy. So, we discourage using stretching altogether; but, if you insist: use whole (integer) ratios of frame-size/ picture-size.

⫸ In order to avoid distortion as a result of stretching, E-Prime 2 now allows you to stretch images while maintaining their aspect ratio. Let's say you want to stretch an image that is 400 x 200 pixels to a size of 100 x 100. Usage of Stretch Mode LeftRight will adjust the width (400) to the new size (100), thus dividing both width and height by four (the image will be 100 x 50 pixels). Conversely, the UpDown Stretch Mode will adjust the height (200) to the new size, thus transforming the image to a 200 x 100 pixels image. Stretch Mode Both is the classic, image-distorting function that divides the width in our example by four, but the height by two.

Transparency (not unlike Harry Potter's invisibility cloak) can be realised by fiddling around with the *Source Color Key, BackColor* and *BackStyle*. In the example, the same image is used as in the previous figure, but the Source Color Key was set to *white*, and BackColor was set to *blue*. As a result, all pixels that were white are now blue. If BackStyle was set to *transparent* instead of *opaque*, all the blue that is shown now would show the previously presented image. Note that none of this is actually reflected in the working area whilst working in E-Studio, but gets applied online, i.e. only when running the actual experiment.

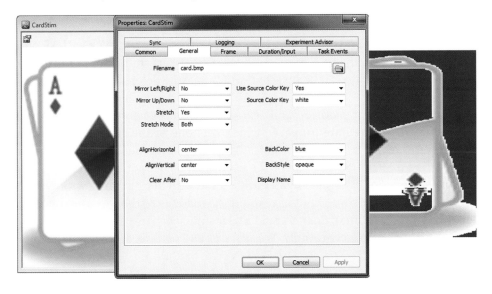

Importantly, when you want to show images in an E-Prime® experiment, these images should be saved in the same folder as the experiment. You can also save images in a separate folder, but in that case you have to specify the path in the filename field, which will almost inevitably lead to confusion when trying to run the experiment from somewhere else (e.g. the lab).

Showing multiple images and layers of texts

If E-Prime® would allow only text *or* images to be displayed on the screen, the program's use would be seriously limited. Luckily, it is also possible to combine text, images, sound and video (see Chapter III) in a single object, called the **Slide**. The Slide is actually a bit like a digital book. It contains one or more states that are like the pages in a book in that they can hold content in a certain layout (which E-Prime® calls the 'frame'). Such content can be text, audio, images, you name it. For example, state one, named 'won', may contain both an image of a smiling face and the text 'you won', whereas state two, named 'lost', may contain both an image of a weeping face and the text 'you lost'.

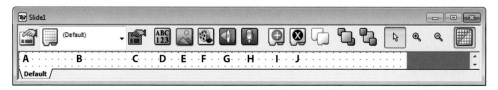

Above, the upper part of a Slide is shown. By clicking on icon **A**, you can edit the properties of the Slide object. Icon **B** enables you to select a *sub-object* you placed on the Slide (e.g. a text object), by clicking on icon **C** you can edit the properties of the *selected sub-object*. To insert a frame where text can be entered, click on **D**. Icon **E** allows you to insert an image, **F** to insert video, **G** to insert sound, and **H** to record sound. With **I**, a new state can be inserted, which may be deleted by clicking on **J**.

You can show different pictures and text using different states. This requires working with the **ActiveState** property, which sets one of the states you made as visible. When working with various states, the idea is that the ActiveState should either refer to an attribute (see one of the exercises) or be manually adjusted just before it is shown. For example, if you have a Slide with a 'right' and 'wrong' state that comes in just after some kind of response is made (say, the Stroop stimulus), you could write a little bit of code to read the accuracy of the Stroop stimulus and then set the ActiveState accordingly. We will discuss reading and writing properties in later chapters.

Feedback

Much easier than the previous example, however, would be to use a **FeedbackDisplay**. FeedbackDisplays are largely the same as Slides; that is, they inherit most, if not all, of the characteristics of Slides, but have some pre-programmed content.

They have four states, and depending on the reaction to *some other object*, the ActiveState is set to one of four states: *Correct, Incorrect, Pending* or *NoResponse*. A common mistake is to forget that FeedbackDisplays need an input object: without that, it *will not work*.

Below, you can see how this works: the FeedbackDisplay1 follows directly after the TargetStimulus and also has this *TargetStimulus* as its *Input Object Name*. Please note that, much like Slides, you will have to edit the properties of the Feedback-Display itself, not one of its four states; so you have to change what was **F** in the previous picture to reflect the exact name of the FeedbackDisplay.

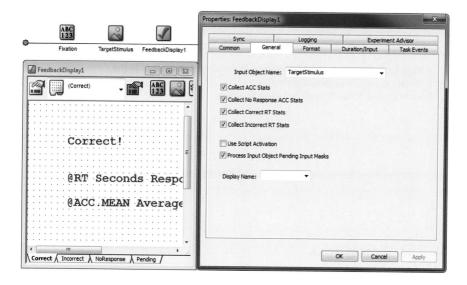

The FeedbackDisplay shows quite a bit of feedback – too much if you ask us! You can and should always accommodate these Slides to better match your specific paradigm and aesthetics. For instance, you may decide to *only* show positive and negative feedback during the training, but following these trials, only show negative feedback and blank screens instead of positive feedback.

You may be wondering, how do the specific states reflect the type of response to the TargetStimulus?

Correct: When the reaction was both fast enough (.RT < .TimeLimit) and correct (.ACC = 1).

Incorrect: When the reaction was fast enough (.RT < .TimeLimit) but incorrect (.ACC = 0).

NoResponse: When there was no reaction, or it was too late (.RT > .TimeLimit). Unless the FeedbackDisplay starts before the .TimeLimit is over: if a participant is given say, three seconds to respond but the FeedbackDisplay starts after one second, it will default to NoResponse as well.

(*Pending*: According to the E-Prime® 'Reference Guide', this option is reserved for future use).

▥➡ Note: If you don't specify the object that the FeedbackDisplay needs to give feedback on, you'll receive the following error message:

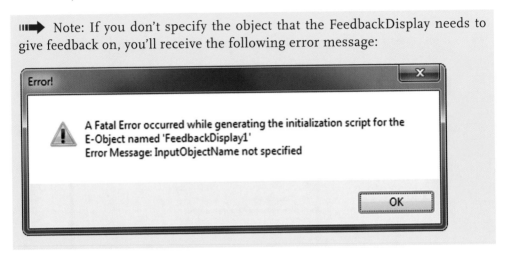

Tutorial II: The Simon Task

J. Richard Simon was interested in hemispheric dominance for speech (left hemisphere for language, and so forth), but found, quite by accident (Simon & Rudell, 1967) a stimulus-response compatibility effect that later became one of the most popular psychological effects after Stroop (1935). He (and Rudell) found that when participants were asked to respond with a left key-press to a command in the left ear, they were much faster than when they were asked to respond with a right key-press to a command in the left ear. This effect, which was then referred to as 'reaction towards the source', was replicated in the visual domain as well, and generally became known as the **Simon Effect**.

In this replica of the visual Simon task, you will learn about working with images, Slides and feedback, as well as using attributes to manipulate variables.

Step 1: Building the basic design

- Begin by building a design similar to the previous tutorial. This means the highest level in the hierarchy, the session Procedure, should have a BlockList, where the two rows each refer to a different Procedure: TrainingProc and TestingProc, for instance. These two Procedures should both get a List: TrainingTrialList and TestingTrialList, where each level refers to the same Procedure: TrainingTrialProc and TestingTrialProc. So, the really stereotypical hierarchy of your experiment should look like the image on the right:

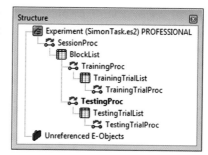

- Now, which latent and manifest variables do we have in this experiment? As the introduction implied, there is a compatibility effect when the *location* of the stimulus differs from the *location* of the response. We can call the only latent variable something like 'compatibility' then: *compatible* if the location of stimulus is equal to the location of the response, and *incompatible* if not. So, we have two manifest variables: StimulusLocation and ResponseLocation and if both have two categories (left and right), the List should contain four (2 x 2) rows. Edit both Lists to accomplish this:

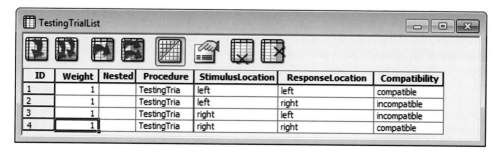

ID	Weight	Nested	Procedure	StimulusLocation	ResponseLocation	Compatibility
1	1		TestingTria	left	left	compatible
2	1		TestingTria	left	right	incompatible
3	1		TestingTria	right	left	incompatible
4	1		TestingTria	right	right	compatible

- Don't forget to save your experiment!

Step 2: Drawing your stimuli

- Since our experiment is only about the visual domain, we can't just use audio files like Simon did, but we still need to cue participants to respond with a left- or right key-press. Usually (and based on later work by Simon), this is done with colours: first, you tell participants to respond with a left key-press whenever they see a blue square, and right if the square is red; and to ignore the location of the square. However, it takes less training to ask participants to respond in the direction indicated by a little arrow. So, we are going to draw arrows.

- Open *MSPaint* (e.g. press 'Start', type in mspaint, press enter). Earlier versions of Paint are slightly different in operation, but the software is so exceedingly simple that this demonstration can easily be extrapolated to operating systems of the past. In MSPaint (Windows 7 version), go to *View*, turn on *Rulers* and drag the lower right corner of the screen around until the image is 100 x 100 pixels. Zoom in to 300% to make sure you have got it right.

- Go to the Home tab and, under *Shapes*, select the rectangle. Draw a square of 50x50 in size, starting at pixel {0, 25}. You can check this in the lower-left corner of the screen or using the rulers. Then, using the line shape, draw lines successively from {50, 0} to {99,49}, from {99, 50} to {50, 99}, and from {50, 99} to {0, 50}. Then, select the paint bucket under Tools and fill the triangle with the colour black. Sit back and reflect upon the beautiful, symmetric simplicity of the end-result in all its wonderful *prägnanz*!

- Save this file to disk, in exactly the same folder where you saved the Simon experiment, as 'ArrowRight.bmp'. Flip your image in Paint in the home tab, using *Rotate > Flip Horizontal*. Then save your picture as ArrowLeft.bmp.

Step 3: Programming the trial

- First, a black fixation cross was presented in the centre of the grey screen for 1000 ms, followed by the presentation of the arrow left (halfway between the left edge and the centre of screen) or right (halfway between the centre and the right edge of the screen). The stimulus remained for 1000 ms on screen, or until the participant responded. A blank screen of 1000 ms was shown after that, unless the response was late or incorrect, in which case the blank screen showed the word 'WRONG!'

- The above is written in more or less the same style you may know from experimental psychological papers. Both now and during the examination, you will try to replicate this Procedure.

- Create a fixation mark as in the previous tutorial, but on a grey background and with a duration of 1000 ms.

- Insert a Slide and insert an image frame within the Slide. Change the following properties: 1) The image's FileName: ArrowRight.bmp; 2) The image's Width: 100; Height: 100 (in pixels!); 3) Position: X: 25%; Y: 50%; 4) Use Source Color: Yes. Key: White. BackColor: Grey; 5) The state's Background Color: Grey.

- Now, if you try to run your experiment, you should see an arrow pointing right on the left side of the screen. This stands to reason, since we requested the ArrowRight.bmp to be presented at 25% of the screen, but we want the List to sometimes pick, for example, ArrowLeft.bmp to be presented at 75% of the screen. [The moral here should be clear: when you try to get at least one of the conditions to work (an arrow pointing right presented left), it should be far easier to figure out *where exactly those attributes go*.]

- So, edit your Lists and add one attribute, CorrectResponse. Then, rename your attribute ResponseLocation to ArrowFileName. For every StimulusLocation that is left, insert 25%, right 75%. For every ArrowFileName, make it say either ArrowLeft.bmp or ArrowRight.bmp. For ArrowFileName that say ArrowLeft.bmp or ArrowRight.bmp, make the CorrectResponse 'q' or 'p', respectively:

- Change the image's filename to [ArrowFileName] and its location to [StimulusLocation]. Change the properties of the Slide *itself*: the duration should be 1000, the input device should be a keyboard, the allowable responses are 'qp' and the correct response is [CorrectResponse].

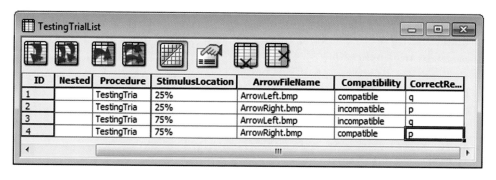

ID	Nested	Procedure	StimulusLocation	ArrowFileName	Compatibility	CorrectRe...
1		TestingTria	25%	ArrowLeft.bmp	compatible	q
2		TestingTria	25%	ArrowRight.bmp	incompatible	p
3		TestingTria	75%	ArrowLeft.bmp	incompatible	q
4		TestingTria	75%	ArrowRight.bmp	compatible	p

▮▮▮➡ Instead of using the filename including its extension, you can also omit the '.bmp' in the List and simply use 'ArrowLeft' and 'ArrowRight' as values of the attribute ArrowFileName. In that case, make sure to refer to the image's filename as '[ArrowFileName].bmp'. E-Prime® will now automatically append '.bmp' to the value of the attribute.

- Add a FeedbackDisplay after the Simon stimulus, and set its *Input Object Name* to be that Simon stimulus. Clear all text from all four states, add the text 'Wrong' in the *Incorrect* and *NoResponse* states and set background of all four states to grey.

- Finished! Check the experiment, see if it compiles and runs okay.

Exercises

- Also, check whether data is saved and if you would actually be able to analyse it. The Simon effect should show about 30 ms longer reaction times with incompatible trials.

- Extend the current design with a *training* List.

- Using single-state Slides, make an introduction-, an instruction- and a good-bye screen.

- Instead of manipulating the direction of the arrow (the target) by letting an attribute refer to the target's filename, you can also make clever use of the target Slide's ActiveState property. Let ActiveState refer to an attribute in the List and try to get the experiment to work.

- So, what does the Simon effect *mean*? Simon himself figured that the location of the stimulus, even though it is completely irrelevant to the task, automatically triggers a response towards that stimulus; much like you will look over your right shoulder if someone taps on it. If that is true, it may also be true that the more peripheral a visual stimulus is presented, the stronger a reaction towards that location will be triggered. Design an experiment to test the following hypothesis: more peripheral stimuli elicit greater Simon effects than more central stimuli. Use at least three distances, for example 25%, 35% and 45% for left vs. 55%, 65% and 75% for right responses.

Tutorial III: Implicit Association Task

The Implicit Association task (IAT) has been designed to measure implicit attitudes and beliefs that people are unwilling to report (Greenwald et al., 1998). In this tutorial you will program a gender-career IAT. This task may reveal that there are implicit associations between family and females and between career and males. The typical IAT Procedure consists of a series of five discrimination tasks (Greenwald et al., 1998). A pair of target concepts and an attribute dimension are introduced in the first two steps. Categories for each of these discriminations are assigned to a left or right response. These are combined in the third step and then recombined in the fifth step, after reversing response assignments (in the fourth step) for the target-concept discrimination. If there are implicit associations, responses in the 5th block should be faster than responses in the 3rd block with the reverse mapping.

The table below shows whether the left- or the right hand response (indicated by an asterisk at the left or the right side of the category) should be mapped to the respective category (cf. Greenwald et al., 1998; Figure 1 therein).

Sequence	1	2	3	4	5
Task description	Initial target-concept discrimination	Associated attribute discrimination	Initial combined task	Reversed target-concept discrimination	Reversed combined task
Task instruction	* Male Female *	* Family Career *	* Male * Family Female * Career *	Male * * Female	Male * * Family * Female Career *

Step 1: Building the basic design

- Begin by making a BlockList where the five rows refer to the five blocks described above. LeftLabel and RightLabel refer to the response-mapping.

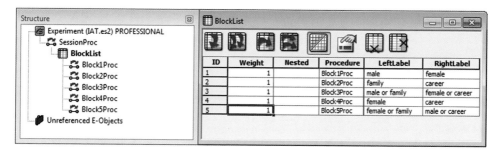

- Don't forget to save your experiment.

- Add a List to Block1Proc and name this List 'Block1List'. Edit Block1List to make it look like this List:

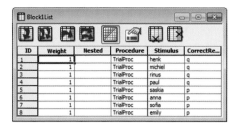

In the column CorrectResp a "q" refers to a LeftLabel stimulus and a "p" to a Right-Label stimulus.

- Add BlockLists to the other four BlockProcedures in a similar way. In block 2 the stimulus column should contain only career and family related words; in block 3 the stimulus column should contain both names and career and family related words, etc.

Step 2: Programming the trial

- Create a fixation screen with a duration of 1000 ms.

- Make a Slide called 'TargetStimulus' on which you use three TextObjects to present the attributes: LeftLabel, RightLabel and Stimulus. LeftLabel should be presented in the upper left corner, RightLabel should be presented in the upper right corner and Stimulus should be presented in the centre. Look back to Chapter 1 to see how you can specify on the frame tab where on the screen a frame is presented.

- Set the duration to 1500 ms, specify the allowable response keys as 'pq' and refer to the attribute *CorrectResp* to specify the correct response.

- Run your experiment and check if everything is presented in the correct position on the screen.

Exercises

- Add an instruction screen to the experiment.

- Check your own implicit attitudes. Are you faster in block 5 (where male and career, and female and family require the same response), compared to block 3 (in which male and family, and female and career require the same response)?

- Add a FeedbackDisplay with a duration of 1500 ms to the trial Procedure. Adjust the FeedbackDisplay so that it only gives feedback when you make an error, otherwise it should just show a blank screen.

Advanced Exercises

Try to program the Stroop task described in this chapter yourself. Instead of using only red and green, add blue as a third colour. In your experiment you should have nine different combinations:

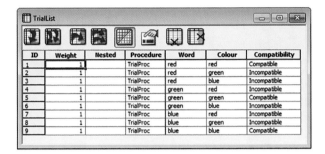

ID	Weight	Nested	Procedure	Word	Colour	Compatibility
1	1		TrialProc	red	red	Compatible
2	1		TrialProc	red	green	Incompatible
3	1		TrialProc	red	blue	Incompatible
4	1		TrialProc	green	red	Incompatible
5	1		TrialProc	green	green	Compatible
6	1		TrialProc	green	blue	Incompatible
7	1		TrialProc	blue	red	Incompatible
8	1		TrialProc	blue	green	Incompatible
9	1		TrialProc	blue	blue	Compatible

Make sure, however, that compatible trials occur as often as incompatible trials!

Chapter III

Sound, movies, hardware, and nested Lists

In this chapter, you will learn

About:
- The SoundOut object
- Digital audio
- The MovieDisplay object
- The Wait object
- The Label object
- Experiment Properties
- Nested Lists, and
- Counterbalancing and between-subjects manipulations

How to:
- Replicate a visual search experiment
- Program an ego depletion experiment, and
- Jitter inter-trial intervals (ITIs) using nested Lists

In this chapter you will learn how to make a *visual search experiment* (i.e. looking for letters in a String) and, additionally, how to add annoying sounds to that task in order to compare those distracting sounds' effects when cognitive load is high or low. As always, we start this chapter by describing the basic elements of the objects and elements used in the experiments (particularly the sound object) and in addition you will (finally?) be able to impress your friends by acquiring this chapter's wisdom regarding what **bit-depth** and **sample rate** actually are (two terms which are always used but poorly understood). You will be shown how to counterbalance blocks, use **nested Lists** and use **jitter** (nice Scrabble word!) to create more advanced experimental designs. In addition, we show you how to add devices to your experiment and you will be taught the **Match Desktop Resolution At Runtime** option which can be helpful if you run the same experiment on different PCs. We understand that you are impatient to get started, therefore, without further ado, let's talk about SoundOut objects and digital audio.

SoundOut objects and digital audio

Since the nineteenth century, psychoacoustics has, sadly, no longer been a major part of universities' psychology curriculum. For this reason, one may argue that much less is known about the auditory system compared with the visual one, which should, in itself, be enough reason to go ahead and study the perception of sound. Still, if you have less ambitious plans, sound can be pretty useful as a way, for example, to present feedback (e.g. a sharp, loud beep if the participant reacts incorrectly or when your bank account hits zero). After you have read this chapter's section on sound, you should be able to avoid the most common errors, and know the basics about digital audio. As a starter, let's talk about how to insert sound in E-Prime®.

SoundOut Objects

As you may have come to expect, a **SoundOut** object can be inserted into a Procedure as well as into a Slide in much the same way as TextDisplays and ImageDisplays. However, E-Prime® will not run if the **SoundDevice** is not activated. You can check whether the SoundDevice is activated by following these steps: *Edit > Experiment > Devices*. The SoundDevice is activated when *Sound* is selected.

With E-Prime 2, the implementation of the SoundDevice has changed to an impressive degree, allowing different formats (.mp3, .wma) and drivers.

E-Prime 1

Prior to the production release of E-Prime 2, E-Studio could still crash if you were not very careful when choosing your acoustic stimuli. The reason is that E-Prime® expected your .wav (Windows default uncompressed audio) files or other sound files (e.g. mp3) to be of a specific format. For those using older versions of E-Prime®, you can go to SoundDevice: *Edit > Experiment > Devices > Sound > Edit* and see the screen to the left. The **wave files** in your experiment should all conform to the values entered in the SoundDeviceObject Properties. Exactly *what* these properties refer to will be discussed in the section on digital audio, whereas *how* to adjust your audio files so that they can actually be played in E-Prime® will be shown in this chapter's tutorial. Meanwhile, in E-Prime 1, *if the audio files are not of the sample-rate defined here*, E-Prime® aborts.

E-Prime 2

If you have E-Prime 2, going to *Edit > Experiment > Devices > Sound > Edit* should bring up the screen to the right. Here, we find that the sample-rate and bit-depth of a file is no longer important – or at least, failure to comply will no longer result in a crash – but users are asked to make a choice between various drivers. The one shown here, DirectSound, is a software component of Microsoft DirectX technology, which has as a main advantage that it will work with pretty much any audio interface that is running on your computer (your PC's audio hardware). The disadvantage is that the delay between the moment your PC is

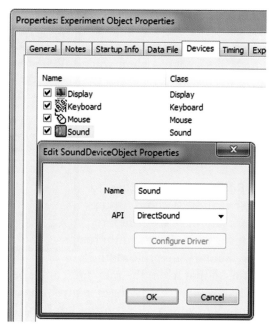

commanded to 'play a sound', and the actual time the audio is heard can be long. Other drivers are available that effectively circumvent the normal route from software, through intermediary layers of the Windows operating system, to the sound card and thereby reduce the latency involved considerably. ASIO, for example, is a computer sound card driver protocol developed by Steinberg, and is the same weapon of choice for producers and sound engineers who use professional audio software like Cubase. The problem is that your audio interface may not have such a driver (but search the internet for ASIO4ALL). To test and configure this, simply open the Sound Tester in the E-Prime 2 folder in the start menu and follow the instructions.

Back to any type of E-Prime®

...in which we assume that you have successfully configured your driver (E-Prime 2) or that chimes.wav file was in fact a 2 channel, 22050 samples, 16 bit file (it was not!). In order to make E-Prime® play this file, the following properties of the SoundOut object are relevant:

A. The **Filename** should refer to a valid .wav file that is preferably located within the directory where the experiment was last saved. Also, much like images, when you want to copy or move the experiment, you will also have to copy the sounds that are used in your experiment to this new folder.

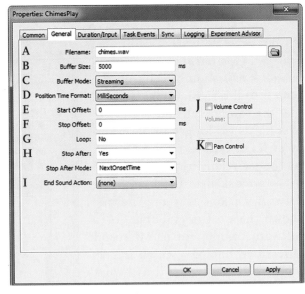

B. **Buffer Size**. In order to present audio without timing errors (latency), E-Prime® reserves a part of the computer's memory to preload the audio, so that when the moment comes to start this audio file, E-Prime® can immediately play it. This ought to give you some peace of mind regarding the timing accuracy of your audio stimuli, but it is always best to check this yourself. If you still use E-Prime 1, our advice would be to make the buffer's maximum length just a little bit longer (in milliseconds) than the longest audio file you will present. In E-Prime 2, it is probably best to set the Buffer Mode to Streaming (below), and set Buffer Size to a *low* value, unless you start hearing artefacts (mentioned below).

C. The **Buffer Mode** property can be set to 'Buffered' and 'Streaming'. In 'Buffered' mode the maximum length of the sound file will be the maximum length supported by the hardware buffer of the sound card. The 'Streaming' mode enables a much longer length of an audio file, but may result in timing issues if Buffer Size is too low, due to the asynchronous loading and playing processes (like watching YouTube on a slow internet connection). In general, Streaming Mode is more flexible and possibly preferable, whereas Buffered Mode is provided mainly for backward compatibility with E-Prime 1.

D. In the **Position Time Format** property the format of the **Start Offset** and **Stop Offset** properties can be selected. The following formats are available: Milliseconds, Microseconds and Bytes.

E. **Start Offset** is the moment within the buffer from which to play the audio. So: if your buffer is (partly) filled with audio file 'chimes.wav' (a default Windows file) and you have the Start Offset set at 300, the first 300 ms of the sound are skipped.

F. **Stop Offset** is the moment within the buffer where the audio stops playing. So: if your buffer is (partly) filled with audio file 'chimes.wav', and the Stop Offset is set at 350, the audio stops playing after 350 ms.

G. Setting the **Loop** property of a SoundOut object to *Yes* makes the audio file repeat (through the buffer) for as long as the duration of the stimulus.

H. By setting **Stop After** to 'No', the audio keeps playing even if the SoundOut object is no longer 'present', so that you can still hear the sound whilst the rest of your experiment continues. That is: if you have the SoundOut Object's duration set at 200 ms, the Stop After Mode to the default NextOnsetTime and the stop offset at 800 ms, the sound will play for a further 600 ms while the next object is already running. This is particularly useful if you want to use SoundOut objects but you want to present them simultanepously with other stimuli or reactions.

I. Using **End Sound Action**, it is possible, after the sound file ends, to skip to the next object (by selecting *Terminate*) or let the experiment jump to a Label.

J. With **Volume Control**, you can edit the volume of the sample 'ad hoc': by entering a value of -10,000, the sound becomes attenuated for about 100 dB (which usually makes it silent). By entering a value of -5000, the sound becomes 50 dB softer, and so forth. The sound can't be made *louder* using this volume control, only softer.

K. **Pan Control** works similarly to Volume Control. By entering a value of -10,000, the right channel is attenuated by 100 dB, so that only the left channel is audible; a value of 10,000 makes the left audio-channel 100 dB softer, so that only the right side is playing. Since this pan control only attenuates one channel, it is necessarily so that audio in the centre (with both left and right playing) sounds louder to the human ear than sounds that are panned, confounding panning with volume. If you don't want this, please look up 'panning laws' on the internet.

Digital audio

So, what is this sample rate and bit depth? Why can't E-Prime 1 play chimes.wav without changing the properties of the SoundDevice? How do we present a 70 dB sound?

All these questions are related to the specialist realm of digital audio. The waveform of air that is sound can be *approximated* by digital computers using bits.

That is, every so many microseconds, as specified by a file's sample-rate, the value of the waveform is specified with a finite number of bits, as illustrated below.

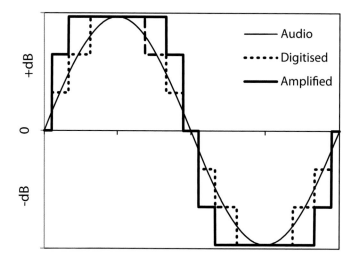

Imagine we have been granted seven distinct values to represent analogue sound to the best of our abilities. Thus the hair-line above ('analogue audio') becomes transformed to the seven integers (-3 to +3). Obviously, both having more samples per second (i.e. times the number is transcribed horizontally in the graph above), as well as having more bits per sample (number of different values available, or what is the vertical resolution in the graph above), makes our digital approximation closer to reality. In other words, sample-rate and bit-depth increase the precision of our digital representation. As can be seen, having the seven values allows us to describe the waveform up to a value of 3, which then becomes an absolute ceiling level of amplitude. This is okay because when using digital or any other kind of amplified audio, the audio level (in dB) is always relative to the listener and the amplifier; indeed, the same chimes.wav played over the audio system at a rock festival sounds quite a bit louder than when played over Michiel's LCD screen at the office. Digital audio can, however, have a maximum of amplitude: that is 3 (or -3) in our case, since we lack the bits to describe the waveform going higher. Thus, the result of amplifying our sample using software results in the thick line above. Since no more bits are available to represent the waveform over and above the level of 3 (-3), the waveform becomes flat at the peaks. If you translate this back into the analogue domain, the result is a fair bit of pretty nasty noise. Therefore, in digital audio, sound is described as having a maximum level of 0 dB, but having a minimum level of $-\infty$ dB.

To summarise:

Resolution in digital audio is defined both by its *sample rate* and its *bit-depth*.

- The sample rate refers to the number of moments in time in which the value of the waveform is described; CDs typically have a sample rate of 44,100, DVDs 48,000.

- The bit-depth refers to the number of bits used to measure the value of the waveform; CDs typically have bit-depths of 16, DVDs 24.

- You can't ask E-Prime® to present a 70 dB sound; but you can amplify a digital sound that has a peak value of 0dB to 70 dB. To measure audio levels in your experiment, look for a digital ear or similar device.

MovieDisplay object

A MovieDisplay object can be inserted on a Procedure as well as on a Slide in the same way as TextDisplays, Image-Displays and SoundOut objects. With the MovieDisplay object you can present digital video with the following formats: DivX, Xvid, MPEG-1, MPEG-2, MPEG-4, H-264 and WMV.

On the General tab of the properties window of the MovieDisplay the file-name of the movie to be presented can be specified. As is the case with images, movies should be saved in the same folder as your experiment, unless the complete path is specified in the **File-name** property.

Start Position uses a MovieTimeFrame to set the starting position of the movie. MovieTimeFrame is specified in hours, minutes, seconds, milliseconds.

Stop Position uses a MovieTimeFrame to set the stop position of the movie.

Stop After determines whether the movie has to stop playing when the object ends (i.e. similar to the SoundOut object).

Stretch determines whether the movie has to be stretched or cropped to fit the frame size. (i.e. similar to the SoundOut object).

End Movie Action can terminate the MovieDisplay upon the end of the file, or alternatively jump to a Label.

Films are created by rapidly showing a number of images (frames) each second. In the US this 'frame-rate' is about 24/second, in Europe, about 25. The MovieDisplay object has several unique logging options relating to frames:

Sync	Logging

Property Logging

Check the items to have their values logged in the context

	Property Name	Category ▽
☐ ●	ACC	Dependent Measures
☐ ●	CRESP	Dependent Measures
☐ ●	RESP	Dependent Measures
☐ ●	RT	Dependent Measures
☐ ●	RTTime	Dependent Measures
☐ ●	Tag	General
☐ ○	FirstFrameTime	Movie
☐ ○	FrameRate	Movie
☐ ○	FramesDisplayed	Movie
☐ ○	FramesDropped	Movie
☐ ●	DurationError	Time Audit
☐ ●	OnsetDelay	Time Audit
☐ ●	OnsetTime	Time Audit
☐ ●	OnsetToOnset...	Time Audit

FirstFrameTime: Presentation time (ms) of the first frame time stamped to the beginning of the experiment.

FrameRate: Number of frames per second.

FramesDisplayed: Number of frames displayed.

FramesDropped: Number of frames dropped.

Wait object

The **Wait** object ⌛ is very similar to the Text- and ImageDisplays except that it doesn't show anything, i.e. it doesn't overwrite preceding screen content. You can also use Wait objects to do most of the other stuff that is available in TextDisplays, such as logging responses. Response logging might be useful in the rare case where you want the display to show the content presented by the previous object (the screen is not cleared yet), e.g. until a response has been given in the current Wait object. See, for instance, tutorial VIII step 3 for an implementation of the Wait object.

Labels

The **Label** 🚩 is more than a pretty banner to brighten up your E-Studio, but not a lot more. In programming, it is merely a defined moment in the script. One foible of the **Basic** programming language – which has close links with E-Prime® – is that one can skip lines of programming using the **Goto** statement. On the Commodore 64, the Childhood Sweetheart of at least one of the authors, for example, the following would produce the text 'Hello' on the screen:

```
10 Print "Hello"
20 End
```

... but, the C=64 fan's heart would start pounding faster with the following mini-program, which greets the aspiring programmer until the end of days:

```
10 Print "Hello"
20 Goto 10
30 End
```

In later versions of Basic, the line numbers were not required in code anymore (because it is pretty annoying to recode all the numbers when you want to insert a piece of code!), but the Goto statement remained in vogue:

```
BeforeHello:
Print "Hello"
Goto BeforeHello
End
```

...would still produce our enthusiastic greeting. So, in E-Prime®, these Labels can be inserted onto timelines, much like objects, but they are represented in the E-Prime® script as nothing more than the name of the Label with a colon added to it.

You can use such Labels for two reasons. First, as said and as will be explained later on, it can be used in programming (InLine scripts). Second, all objects in E-Prime® that can capture responses (such as the TextDisplay, etc.) provide a way to jump to the Label. When you enter the name of a Label in a **Jump Label** property of an object and set the *End Action* to *Jump* (both in the *Duration/Input* tab), the participant is moved *forwards or backwards in time*, so to speak. That is, all objects between the current one and the Label to which to jump are then skipped. For an example, see Chapter V (Solution 1) or how we have used Labels in Tutorial VIII.

One word of caution though: it is only possible to jump to a Label *within the same Procedure*. It is possible to skip Lists and then jump to a Label on a higher level, for example, but it takes a bit of programming (described in the E-Basic help under FactorSpace.Terminate, see also Chapter V). Also, the use of Goto statements tend to result in very opaque code: we go from this bit to that, jump over and sideways, up and down the code, in a pattern that has aptly been named 'spiderweb' or 'spaghetti' code amongst coders of other programming languages. Often, use of *Goto* can and should be avoided.

Experiment properties

Since we have already mentioned how to activate the SoundDevice by going to *Edit > Experiment > Devices*, we might as well name a few more useful things in the experiment properties. Basically, this is the place where you set and edit properties that are constant throughout the experiment, such as which **Startup** info to ask the experimenter (or the participant) and which hardware devices to use. The other tabs of the experiment properties are not mentioned since they are either too self-explanatory or too advanced. As a result, we seldom use those tabs.

Startup Info

When you run an experiment, E-Prime® by default asks you which participant number and session number it should use. Since these values are immediately logged, it is pretty useful to add more prompts like this to the start-up info: age, sex, and handedness, for example. To do this, you can either click on *Add* and make a new one, or use one of the current prompts by clicking on the checkbox next to one *and then* selecting this

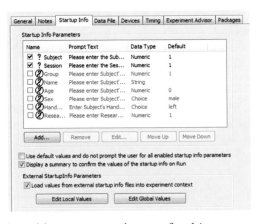

Startup parameter, clicking on *Edit*, and enabling *Prompt the user for this startup info parameter*. It seems rather redundant that E-Prime® allows you to add these parameters without actually using them in the experiment, but it is certainly flexible.

Devices

Like the SoundDevice, other hardware devices can also be inspected, added, removed and edited in the *Experiment>Edit>Devices* screen.

We've already discussed the properties of the SoundDevice. About the others:

- The **keyboard** is on and activated by default. You can also edit several properties, such as whether the Caps Lock is enabled and whether to also collect key-releases (instead of only key-presses).

- The **mouse** is on by default, but the cursor is hidden. This allows you to record mouse button presses. In case you also need a mouse cursor, set Show Cursor to *Yes* and use E-Basic code to determine its location.

- The **Serial port** is an older way of communicating between computers or other hardware, which we sporadically use in the lab since it is relatively easy to connect specialised input devices and because its timing is very accurate.

- The **SRBOX** is PST's own way to collect key-presses and voice-onsets. This is basically an ugly grey box with the name 'Serial Response Box'. It features a 0 millisecond debounce period, something that simply can't be achieved from a standard keyboard. We use it in the lab for two reasons: 1) for button-press requiring extremely precise reaction times or experiments requiring psychophysiological (e.g. **EEG**, electroencephalogram) recordings; and, 2) for experiments that use the microphone to collect reaction times, which we call **voice-key** (typically employed in language production studies and Stroop tasks).

Display hardware

Since this is a subject that is of crucial importance to most psychological experiments, the display properties are treated separately from the rest.

The Display is the screen used to present stuff during experiments. Importantly, you can set the width and height (in pixels) here, as well as the bits used for colours. You will notice the screen looks pretty pixelated when you run an experiment without changing the Display settings; this can be avoided by increasing the width and height, but it will simultaneously make everything appear smaller. While many CRT monitors have a display with a resolution of 1280 x 1024 pixels, E-Prime's display is set to 640 x 480 by default. This makes everything you see on screen whilst designing your experiment look about twice as large when you run it. So, in order to prevent confusion, you may set the option *Match Desktop Resolution At Run Time* to *Yes*. An additional advantage of using this option is that E-Prime® doesn't need to adjust the display (preventing technical difficulties). However, note that the desktop resolution on a lab computer is likely to differ from the desktop resolution on the computer where you designed the experiment initially, so it is important to check (and change) the lab computer's desktop resolution before running your experimental sessions.

Generally, every pixel on the screen is updated a number of times every second. This is usually sixty times a second (60 Hz) on **LCD monitors** (*liquid crystal displays*, also known as 'flat-screens'), but higher **refresh rates** can be obtained by using **CRT monitors** (*cathode ray tubes*, also known as 'those old, big things'), which is why psychologists still use these in their labs. Basically, the refresh rate is the final boundary of timing accuracy: if a screen is updated sixty times a second, this means every pixel is at least shown for 1000 / 60 = 16.67 milliseconds. Ergo: on LCD screens it is impossible to show a stimulus for, say, 15 ms. More importantly: it is impossible to show a pixel for 95 ms, for instance, and a timing error would result from attempting this (16.67 x 5=83.33 whereas 16.67 x 6=100). However, some old CRT monitors can have refresh rates of 160 Hz, one update every 6.25 ms, so we could theoretically show both primes lasting a mere 6.25 ms and show a pixel for about 94 ms; but: *the higher the resolution*, the longer it takes to update all pixels, and *the lower the refresh rate* (at least for old computer systems). This is the reason why E-Prime® runs at such a low resolution by default.

Timing errors due to refresh rates can be unavoidable. The basic problem is that although stimuli can be shown independently from the update time, there is no way to know which pixels were updated. For example, the lower part of a stimulus is updated first because the updating 'cycle' was there when the command to show the stimulus on the screen was presented; so, for a brief moment, only a pat of the stimulus is shown (a phenomenon called 'screen tearing'). This makes matters rather confusing to say the least, so it is generally considered good practice to at least time the stimuli so that they are presented just before their turn to show up comes around: this we call 'onset sync'.

Some points:

- Higher resolutions (width x height): smaller, but better quality images.

- For some old computer systems there might be a trade-off between screen resolution and maximum refresh rate: the higher the resolution, the lower the refresh rate.

- Sync display onsets (Onset Sync = vertical blank) and be prepared for timing inaccuracy.

- Always have your experiment's display settings adjusted to your Windows display settings.

- When timing is critical, always check the refresh rate of the monitor before running your experimental session, see *Display.RefreshRate* logging in the edat file and/or use an Inline script that checks the resolution before running your experiment (see the example in Chapter V).

Nested Lists

So far, we have conveniently ignored the Nested property of the List object. If you remember how we explained the degree to which randomisation resembles shuffling a deck of cards, perhaps you will find it convenient to think of a *nested List* as shuffling a stack of cards (containing, say, three Aces) next to our current deck. You can use the Nested property in similarly profitable ways in E-Prime® when organising your experiment. Calling (by writing any name) a List will immediately cause a pre-existing or new List to appear directly underneath the List in which it is mentioned in the Structure Window.

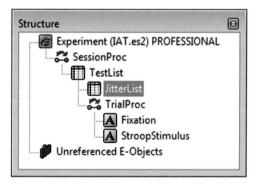

One useful way of using the *Nested* property is to create a *jitter* in your experiment. With a *nested JitterList* you can easily randomise the duration of the fixation display to make the experiment less predictable. In order to create a nested JitterList you type 'JitterList' in the *Nested* column of your experiment List:

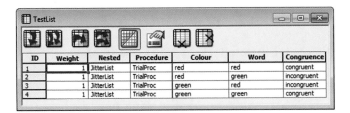

ID	Weight	Nested	Procedure	Colour	Word	Congruence
1	1	JitterList	TrialProc	red	red	congruent
2	1	JitterList	TrialProc	red	green	incongruent
3	1	JitterList	TrialProc	green	red	incongruent
4	1	JitterList	TrialProc	green	green	congruent

Now during every trial, the nested JitterList will be called on and, consequently, a new 'card' is selected from your second stack. In the nested JitterList you can create an Atrribute called 'Jitter':

You can now refer to the attribute *Jitter* in the duration property of your fixation display. If the selection-option *Random* is selected in the nested JitterList, then every time the JitterList is called on, it will randomly select the duration of the fixation display. Note that in the nested List the column Procedure is left blank.

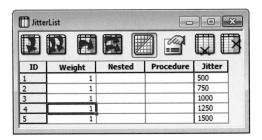

ID	Weight	Nested	Procedure	Jitter
1	1			500
2	1			750
3	1			1000
4	1			1250
5	1			1500

Counterbalancing and between-subject manipulations

When creating experiments, it can be useful to counterbalance instructions, stimuli or response options between subjects. When you do this, half of your participants may receive one instruction, stimulus or response option and the other half of your participants may receive another instruction, stimulus or response option. You can counterbalance by simply creating two different versions of the same experiment. However, in E-Prime® you can also easily counterbalance by using the nice features nested Lists provide!

If, for instance, you want to manipulate instructions between subjects, you add a nested List, let's call it 'CBList', to your main experiment List. In this nested *CBList* you can add an attribute called 'Instruction'. On the *Selection* tab of the CBList properties you select *Counterbalance*. You can now choose whether you want to counterbalance by *Subject*, *Session* or *Group*. In the case of

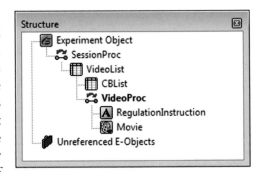

a between-subjects manipulation, you may use the option to counterbalance *Ordered By Group*. In this case, make sure that 'Group' is selected in your *Startup Info* Parameters so that the (non-blinded) experimenter can enter the Group number when running the study.

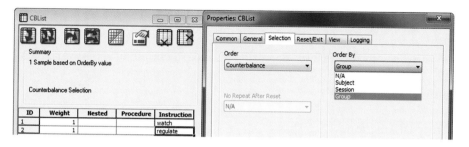

You might also consider to Counterbalance by Subject instead. In case you use two levels in the CBList, level ID 1 will always be selected when running experiments with odd Subject numbers (1, 3, 5, 7, 9 etc.), whereas level ID 2 will always be selected when running experiments with even Subject numbers (2, 4, 6, 8, 10, etc.). Of course, it is possible to add more levels. For example, if you use four levels, level 1 will be selected for Subjects 1, 5, 9; level 2 will be selected for Subjects 2, 6, 10 etc. The counterbalance option uses the modulus function to determine the level. The modulus is the other part of the answer for integer division; it's the remainder. For example, if you divide 208 by 10, the modulus is 8: the part that can't be divided without using fractions.

Tutorial IV: Visual search and distracting sound

Sound can be a joy as well as a nuisance. Today, we will design an experiment that measures the effect of the rather annoying 'Windows Critical Stop' sound on tasks with high and low cognitive load. Intuitively, one would think it is more distracting to hear this nasty sound if you are mentally very active, so we predict a higher effect of distracting sound during tasks with a high cognitive load.

ID	Weight	Nested	Procedure	VisualSearchFinder
1	1			qetuoadgjl
2	1			zcbmadgjlq
3	1			wryipadgjl
4	1			xvnadgjlqe
5	1			adgtlqetip
6	1			sfhwtryipz
7	1			dgjlztbmwr
8	1			fhkzbtmqey

Our experiment will be a classic one, yet again: the *visual search* task (e.g. Duncan & Humphreys, 1989). Basically, we ask participants to search a screen containing distracters (here: all letters except the 't'), and to look for a target (the 't'). Cognitive load is then manipulated by increasing the number of distracters. We require our participants to respond, as fast as possible, by pressing 't' if they find a target, or 'n' if there is no target. The prediction is that, on average, participants will take longer to press 't' when there is a distracting sound, but this effect should be more pronounced when the number of distracters is increased.

Step1: Building the basic design

Let's first think about the design. Basically, we have a couple of latent variables:

- Cognitive Load.

- Auditory Distraction.

But, more importantly, we operationalise these latent variables with manifest variables:

- Target or non-target trial: the trial may either actually contain a target, but half the time (randomised), this is not the case.

- Number of distracters: either 10 or 20.

- Sound: either silence or the Windows Critical Stop.

- And obviously, the response variable: CorrectResponse, which is 't' for target-trials and 'n' for non-target trials. Here is what we made of this 2 x 2 x 2 design:

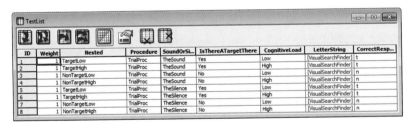

- So, we have a SoundOrSilence attribute, an IsThereATargetThere attribute, the CognitiveLoad attribute and, lastly, the CorrectResponse attribute (derived from IsThereATargetThere). What may not be immediately clear is the use of these *nested* Lists and the *LetterString* attribute. As you can see, we have added four different Lists for each combination of IsThereATargetThere and CognitiveLoad: TargetLow for IsThereATargetThere = Yes and CognitiveLoad = Low, etc. The Letterstring, in turn, refers to an attribute *inside* these different Lists, which is, crucially, named the same between the Lists.

- This, for instance, is our Target-Low List:

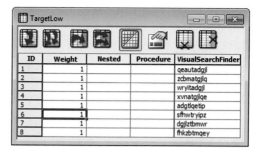

- Notice that the Procedure is always left empty and that the one attribute is called 'VisualSearchFinder', as the Letterstring attribute in the previous List referred to this attribute.

- Our (and your, because we hope you are trying to copy this!) Non-TargetLow List is almost exactly the same: Except, now we have inserted an 'i' for every 't' in the VisualSearchFinder attribute. Therefore, all the words in this List do *not* contain a target, and thus require an 'n' response.

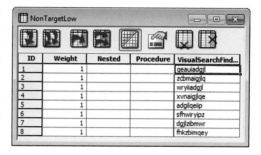

- Do something similar with the TargetHigh and NonTargetHigh Lists (it is possible to copy-paste the cells between Target- and Non-Target Lists and then change all 't's into 'i's), but use more letters.

Once you have done this, and this experiment actually runs, what will happen is this:

- In the first trial, the main List will run the Procedure (TrialProc), and will call upon the TargetLow List to pick a letterstring, which will be retrieved using the VisualSearchFinder attribute, and thus be 'asdfglkjht'. Later on, your participant will be confronted (if you don't randomise) with a string of letters saying 'asdfglkjht', which contains a target and the correct response is therefore 't'.

- In the third trial, the main List will run the Procedure (TrialProc) too, but will call upon the NonTargetLow List to pick a letterstring: 'asdfglkjhi', and so on.

▌▌▶ In fact, the LetterString attribute is, strictly speaking, redundant and added here solely for clarity: the VisualSearchFinder always logs the exact same String. If you prefer to not use the Letterstring attribute, simply refer to the VisualSearchFinder attribute when you need it in the relevant object.

Step 2: Programming the trial

Since this experiment, with four nested Lists, is slightly complicated, let's get the basic task working first. Add a fixation to the beginning of the trial Procedure, then insert a TextDisplay after the fixation and call it something like 'TargetStimulus'. Edit the TargetStimulus' properties

As mentioned previously, in this case it is also correct to refer to [VisualSearch-Finder] instead of [letterstring].

If you did the Lists exactly like us, and inserted these attributes similarly, the experiment should run. Now we only need a bit of sound.

Step 3: Adding sound

Insert a SoundOut object before the TargetStimulus and after the fixation, then edit its properties to the following:

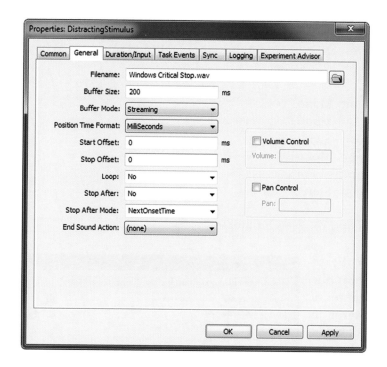

The filename refers to the Windows Critical Stop sound. You can copy this file from your *Windows\Media* folder and save it in your experiment folder.

Also notice that Loop is set to *No* and Stop After is set to *No*. Finally, and though this screenshot doesn't show it, the *Duration* is set to *0* ms.

Of course, we could have used a Slide instead of a separate TextDisplay and SoundOut.

If you still use E-Prime 1, you will have to check whether the properties of the Windows Critical Stop sound correspond to the properties defined in the SoundDevice. Right click on the Windows Critical Stop sound in your Windows File Explorer. Select *Properties*, and see the *Summary* tab in Windows XP or the *Details* tab in Windows 7. Sadly, Windows 7 no longer immediately shows the sample-rate, bit depth and number of channels.

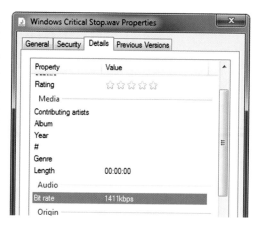

However, for reasons that have been explained earlier, the size of the sample / second (kbps) is a linear function of bit depth, sample-rate and number of channels. Thus:

```
 512kbps =  32kHz  16 bit  Mono
 705kbps =  44kHz  16 bit  Mono
1024kbps =  32kHz  16 bit  Stereo
1058kbps =  44kHz  24 bit  Mono
1152kbps =  48kHz  24 bit  Mono
1411kbps =  44kHz  16 bit  Stereo
```

We thus find that our file is 44 Khz 16 bit Stereo.

Now, you are ready to run the experiment. You should hear the sound-file playing whenever a stimulus is present. However, in half of the trials, no sound should be presented *at all*. Go back to the TrialList, add an attribute called 'VolumeChange' (or any name you prefer) and enter a value of -10,000 for every silent trial (SoundOrSilence = TheSilence) or 0 for every noisy trial (SoundOrSilence = TheSound). In the DistractingStimulus' properties, let the Volume Control's *Volume level* reference the VolumeChange attribute.

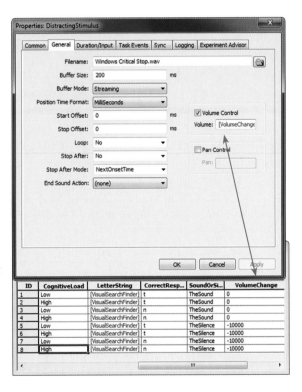

Exercises

- Check your design: is everything randomised correctly?

- Extend the current design with a Training List.

- Make an introduction-, an instruction- and a goodbye screen.

Tutorial V: Ego depletion experiment

The term *ego depletion* refers to the idea that self-control or willpower is a limited resource and, like a muscle, can be fatigued (e.g. Baumeister et al., 1998). Thus, when you put a lot of (mental) effort into a task, this might impair performance on a subsequent task that requires self-control. In this tutorial we are going to test this idea with a simple ego depletion experiment.

The experiment starts with an ego depletion manipulation. In this manipulation one group of participants has to down-regulate their emotions while watching a funny movie (assumed to require self-control), whereas another group of participants can just watch the funny movie without regulation (assumed to require less self-control). Which instruction participants receive will depend on the group number assigned to them. During the second phase of this experiment, participants will perform a demanding task requiring self-control: the Stroop task.

Step 1: Ego depletion manipulation

- Begin by adding a VideoList to the SessionProc. Let the VideoList refer to a VideoProc.

- Don't forget to save your experiment.

- Add a fixation screen (1000 ms) and a MovieDisplay to your VideoProc.

- Edit the MovieDisplay properties as displayed:

The moviefile "PositiveMovie.wmv" can be downloaded from www.e-primer.com and has to be saved in your experiment folder.

End Movie Action is set on "Terminate", this means that the MovieDisplay will disappear once the Movies is finished. Therefore, on the duration tab, you can set the duration property to "infinite".

- Run your experiment and check whether the movie is playing.

- Now it is time to add the ego depletion manipulation. Add a TextDisplay to the VideoProc before the fixation screen. On this TextDisplay you will present the instruction: 'look' for group 1 and 'regulate' for group 2 (more creative instructions allowed). In order to let the instruction differ between the two groups, create a nested CounterBalanceList. Add this nested CounterBalance-List (as is described previously in this chapter) and let your instruction screen refer to the *instruction attribute* that is in your CounterBalanceList.

- Run your experiment and check whether the counterbalancing depends on Group number.

Step 2: Add Stroop task

- Now we are going to add a Stroop task to your experiment. To do this, you start with adding a StroopList with a StroopTaskProc to the SessionProc.

- One of the nice new features of E-Prime 2 is that you can copy parts of experimental Procedures between different experiments. So now you can copy the Stroop task List, which you programmed before, to the StroopTaskProc.

- Run your experiment and check if everything is properly randomised and logged. Run the experiment twice (once for each group) and calculate the Stroop interference effect in both conditions. Is the interference stronger in the situation where you had to control your emotions?

Exercises

- Add a welcome-, instruction- and goodbye screen to your experiment.

- Extend your experiment with a TrainingList.

- Add breaks between the different parts of the experiment.

- Ideally, you would acquire data from two groups (including about 20 individuals each) and perform statistical analyses. Perhaps friends or fellow students can lend a helping hand? Then, merge and analyse your data using E-Merge and E-DataAid.

Advanced excercises

To make an experiment less predictable, you can randomise the duration
of the inter-trial interval (ITI). Add a
nested jitterlist (as described in this
chapter) to the Simon experiment you
created before, to randomise the duration of the ITI.

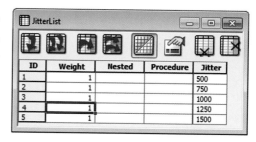

ID	Weight	Nested	Procedure	Jitter
1	1			500
2	1			750
3	1			1000
4	1			1250
5	1			1500

Make sure you understand that the position of where you nest the List matters. Experiment with a nested JitterList in a BlockList instead of a TrialList. What happens?

Chapter IV

Beginning programming in E-Prime®

In this chapter, you will learn

About:
- E-Basic in E-Prime®
- Different types of variables
- Number and String manipulations
- Linking variables to input/output windows
- Linking variables to attributes
- Basic examples to apply InLine scripting

How to:
- Program a working memory test
- Provide feedback on average reaction time and accuracy
- Read and change timing properties in E-Prime®

Always wanted to know if your memory was better than your friend's but never knew how to test that? Don't worry. After this chapter you will finally be able to settle that score once and for all by learning how to program a working memory test. However, in order to do that you will first have to master some of E-Prime's programming language, "E-Basic" (which is mostly outdated Visual Basic). This chapter provides a gentle introduction to Basic programming by introducing several important Basic programming concepts such as "variables", "operators" and "mathematical/String functions". You will further learn how to integrate this programming knowledge into your E-Prime® experiments and finally use it to completely bend E-Prime® to your will. Programming seems difficult and intimidating; however, some things can't be done without some Basic programming knowledge. Rest assured that if you try to read *carefully* through this chapter, read the theory and examples and try the tutorial and exercises, you will be able to do it. If you're stuck with programming though you may always try the very useful E-Prime® online discussion group for more help (http://groups.google.com/group/e-prime/).

E-Basic in E-Prime®

All this dragging about of objects is all fine and dandy, but it doesn't quite feel like programming, does it? According to the developers of the E-Prime® package (PST), E-Prime® doesn't require programming, or "using code". Actually, that is mainly true for tutorial experiments, but rarely for real experiments. Therefore, the remainder of this book is dedicated to giving you a "primer" in E-Prime® code, called **E-Basic** programming, so you can use E-Prime® without running into problems when you want your experiment to be even only slightly different from the standard paradigms.

Whenever you create an experiment in E-Studio and press the *Generate* button, the experiment is *compiled*. This means that the underlying E-Basic code (or script) is generated. This code is displayed in the **Script window**. The Script window has two tabs, a **Full tab** and a **User tab**. The code in the *Full tab* is regenerated each time you press the *Generate* button. You can't change or add anything within this tab, because all the changes are overwritten as soon as the experiment is compiled. If you want to add code, you can do so in two ways; in the *User tab* of the Script window, or in an *InLine object*. The **User Script** on the *User tab* allows you to declare **global variables** (see the next paragraph on Variables and Scope), and to declare functions and subroutines.

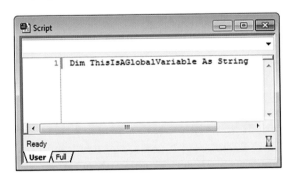

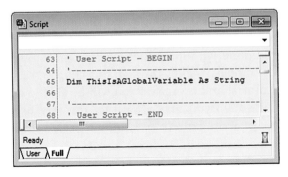

Different types of variables

In programming, a **variable** is a user-defined unit that can have different values. Variables are used to hold some information temporarily (e.g. within a Procedure). You could compare it to variables in mathematical formulas, such as $y = 3x + 5$. In this formula, x and y are variables. By filling in different values for x, y will result in different values. In mathematics, variables are typically numbers. In most programming languages, variables can be of different **types**. For example, an **Integer** can only hold whole numbers. A **Single**, on the other hand, can hold real numbers with 7 decimals. A **Boolean** can be *True* or *False*. A **String** can contain a sequence of characters.

Type	Value	Example
Boolean	True or False	TrainingFinished = true
Integer	Whole numbers, between -32,768 – 32,767	TrialNum = 19
Single	Real numbers (7 digits of precision)	EEGVolt = 0.0000001
String	Text	myName = "Michiel"

So, there are many different types of variables and each can contain some values, but not others. In addition to the four mentioned, more data-types are available in E-Prime®, such as the **Double** (which like a *Single* can hold real numbers, but with 15 decimals), the **Long** (which is like an Integer, but allows higher and lower values) and the **Variant** (which adjusts automatically to whatever it contains). However, being able to use the four types above is usually enough to understand the rest as well.

To use variables, two steps are involved. First, they have to be declared using the **Dim** statement:

```
Dim <new variable name> As <Type>
```

▥➡ The code above shows the **syntax** E-Basic uses. Each programming language has its own spelling and grammar rules. You are assumed to respect them: syntax errors need to be corrected before you can run your experiment.

For example:

```
Dim myName As String
```

Once this is done, E-Basic reserves some memory to contain the value. Also, the Basic language **assigns** a default value (in this case an empty String: "") to your new variable (not in all programming languages), but since you seldom want to use this value, the second step is to assign a value to your variable yourself. For example:

```
myName = "Michiel"
```

To illustrate, let's go back to E-Prime®. In E-Prime®, code may be placed in-between objects by dragging an InLine icon 📄 from the *Toolbox* to a *Procedure*. Double-click it and write down the following:

```
Dim myName As String
myName = "<insert name here>"
Debug.Print myName
```

This piece of code declares the variable myName as a String, then assigns the value "<insert name here>" to it, and finally shows it in the output window of your experiment. When you run this, E-Prime® should show <insert name here> in the Debug tab, which you can find in the bottom part of your screen (press *alt+3* if you don't see this output window).

We use the **Debug.Print** method quite a lot and we think it presents a nifty track that has many uses for debugging your experiment, as it enables you to understand where things went wrong. And during programming, a lot of errors *can* and *will* be made.

Remember, however, that even simple code can disrupt critical timing. If you find you use a lot of Debug.Print during the development phase of your experiment, remember to delete it later on – or at least comment it (so it won't be processed). We found that printing the text "1" to the debug window 100,000 times incurs a delay of about 47 seconds, so the single use of a Debug.Print can cost you 0.47 ms! As a psychologist, your favourite effect may well be in the 30 ms (Simon effect) to 80 ms (Stroop effect) range, so surely, we need not stress how important half a millisecond can be.

Let's now turn to some number variables. Try this in an InLine object:

```
Dim myNumber As Single              'declares myNumber to be a single
Dim myNumberInt As Integer          'declares myNumberInt to be an integer
myNumber = 26.5                     'value 26.5 is assigned to the single
myNumberInt = myNumber              'myNumberInt is assigned the
                                    'value from myNumber

Debug.Print myNumber                'myNumber shown in the debug output.
Debug.Print myNumberInt             'myNumberInt shown in the debug output.
```

What happens here? Notice the **comment** above to see what each line does. All text that is preceded by an apostrophe is ignored by the compiler.

> ➠ A *comment* doesn't form a part of the code. It is used by the programmer to give information about the program. A comment should always be preceded by a single quotation mark (e.g. 'this is a comment). E-Prime® interprets everything after a single quotation mark as comment. In E-Prime 2 you can **comment and uncomment blocks of code** selected in InLine objects using *ctrl+'* and *ctrl+shift+'*.

Let's go back to the code. In the example we have two variables: MyNumber and MyNumberInt. MyNumber gets a value of 26.5, and this value is then copied into myNumberInt. However, since Integers can only be whole numbers, the value is *rounded*. E-Basic differs here from some other programming languages that would cut off, or *truncate*, the part following 26. E-Basic rounds numbers in a rather baffling fashion called "banker's rounding" (or "Dutch rounding"): 26.5 becomes 26, but a 27.5 becomes 28. The logic behind this is that rounding is towards the nearest whole number, *except* in the case of half numbers (at which point the nearest number is at equal distance), in which rounding goes towards the *nearest even* value.

Finally, here is a small consideration regarding case: E-Prime®, and Basic languages in general, doesn't care at all about case. However, we hope you follow us in keeping your case consistent, as failing to do so will make it that much harder to learn languages in which case is important.

Math operators

If you would not do something with a variable, why bother having one? Of course, we call variables "variables" because they can be changed. To change a variable, you simply assign a new value to it. This new value may also be the old value, so logical absurdities like A = A are perfectly okay for most programming languages,

E-Basic included. However, usually we want the value of A to be different. For example, we may perform some **math manipulations** on number variables before the content of a variable is used. E-Basic allows you to apply standard math manipulations using the following **math operators: ˆ (exponentiation), - (negation), * (multiplication), / (division), \ (integer division), mod (modulus division), + (addition), and - (subtraction).** Like in maths, combining operators involves rules of operator precedence. Given that these rules may depend on the programming language you use, it is recommended to always enforce the priority you prefer by using round brackets.

Suppose you would like to calculate the mean reaction time of a participant during a training block. In order to calculate this mean, you need to count the number of trials that have passed during the training block, as well as summate the reaction times across all these trials. After that you divide the summation of reaction times by the number of trials. This will produce the average reaction time during that block.

To illustrate, go back to E-Prime® and program the Simple RT experiment described in Chapter I. Now, let's add an InLine script to the end of the trial Procedure.

In this InLine script, we need three variables. One variable counts the number of trials that have passed and a second variable should summate the RTs across trials. Based on these summations, we can calculate the mean instantly, and this value is stored in the third variable. The content of this third variable is then written to the debugging output.

```
TrialCounter = TrialCounter + 1
RTSummation = RTSummation + TargetStimulus.RT
Dim MeanRT As Single
MeanRT = (RTSummation / TrialCounter)
Debug.Print MeanRT
```

So, in the first line we add 1 to the previous value of TrialCounter. Instead of telling E-Prime® it should add 1 to a variable A, the logical format is this: A = A + 1. Given that the script will run at the end of each trial, we have now created a nice trial counter, which is incredibly useful. The same programming logic is applied to calculate the incremental summation of RTs to the TargetStimulus. (More information about reading properties, such as the RT, of E-Objects will follow later in this chapter.)

However, one important part of the code is still missing. The variables TrialCounter and RTSummation have to be declared first, before they can be used. Unlike the MeanRT variable, which can be declared and used in this InLine script, the summation variables need to be declared at another point in the program. The reason for this is that each time a variable is declared, it will be created anew, and content previously stored in a variable with that same name will be destroyed. Because the counter and summation variables have to store information across trials, they need to be declared on a higher level in the experimental hierarchy. In other words, the **scope** of these variables is different.

▮▮▶ You can only access variables across the entire experiment if you have declared them on the **global level** in the *User Script*. To view the User Script, press *alt+5* (sometimes twice) and click the *User* tab. Everything you declare in the User Script is available throughout your experiment; that is, the scope encompasses the whole experiment. However, note that you can only declare variables there; you can't assign values to them.

So, what we need to do is to open the User Script and add the following lines of code:

```
Dim TrialCounter As Integer
Dim RTSummation As Integer
```

From now on, these variables are available throughout the experiment. If you want to assign initial values to the variables, you have to add an InLine script at the beginning of your SessionProc. Because our counter and sum should start with value 0, we use the following code:

```
TrialCounter = 0
RTSummation = 0
```

Although E-Basic automatically assigns the default value 0 after declaration, it is still good practice to assign the initial value by code yourself. This is because some programming languages simply don't assign a default value to variables at declaration.

Another important point to stress is that the values in RTSummation currently are limited by the range of the Integer data type. Imagine that you would like to use the MeanRT Procedure for more than 100 trials with an average RT of about 400 ms. Because the values in RTSummation now exceeds the value 32,767, a memory overflow will occur and your software may crash. To prevent this error, you would thus need the variable type **Long**, which allows you to store much higher values.

Mathematical functions

Functions are like miniature programs or subprograms/routines that accept data and return a specific result. Like in other software packages, such as Excel or SPSS, E-Basic allows you to use Basic algorithmics as functions in your programming code.

Imagine you would like to obtain the absolute value of x and store the result in variable y. This can be done easily using the **Abs** function:

```
Dim x As Single
Dim y As Single
y = Abs(x)          'returns the absolute value of x and saves the result in y.
```

When you call (execute) a function, you will always need to use the following syntax:

```
<Result_variable> = <Function_Name>(<parameter1>,<parameter2>,etc…)
```

Other examples of math functions are the **Sin()** function, which refers to the arithmetic sine (and not the Original Sin) of a number, and the **Random()** function, which generates a random number (see the ad hoc randomisation example later in this chapter).

Combining numbers and text

Like numbers, text variables also can be manipulated. See the code below:

```
Dim TextStr As String
TextStr = "The mean RT is " & MeanRT
Debug.Print TextStr
```

In this example, the "**&**" **operator** concatenates (i.e. combines) two Strings. Actually, since MeanRT is not a String, it is pretty remarkable that E-Basic can handle this (other languages usually don't allow this). This doesn't always hold, however:

"The mean RT is " is a piece of text; MeanRT is a number, so asking E-Prime® to combine the two is more or less similar to increasing the value of your name by 1, or solving riddles like "Pete / 3 = ?". Should you run into problems like this, E-Prime® will crash and give an 'Error Report' that there was a 'Type Mismatch'. To solve this, you could use the **CStr** function to **convert numerical variables to a String**:

```
<string variable name> = CStr(<numeric variable>)
```

Inversely, to **convert a String to an Integer** you could use the **CInt** function:

```
<integer variable name> = CInt(<string variable>)
```

To **convert a String to a Single**, use **CSng**

```
<single variable name> = CSng(<string variable>)
```

Be careful: Your Windows language settings determine whether "." or "," is interpreted as the decimal separator.

We recommend always using conversion functions and never using E-Basic's implicit conversions. The automatic conversion in E-Basic is not available in most other programming languages, so it is good practice to learn defining variable type conversions explicitly.

So, even though E-Prime® produces the same outcome, it is strongly recommended to use the following code instead of the code described earlier:

```
Dim TextStr As String
TextStr = "The mean RT is " & CStr(MeanRT)
Debug.Print TextStr
```

Or, after applying some **code substitution**, this single line of code will also work fine:

```
Debug.Print "The mean RT is " & CStr(MeanRT)
```

Rather than using the CStr function, you may also be interested in using the **Format()** function. This function allows you to define the format of how the number is converted into text. For instance, this code shows the content of a Single variable with a precision of only 2 decimals (again rounded, not truncated).

```
Debug.Print "The mean RT is " & Format(MeanRT,"0.00")
```

String functions

If you would like to **manipulate the content of a String**, several functions might be useful. The most common functions are listed below.

Len uses this syntax:

```
<integer> = Len(<string>)
```

It counts the number of characters in a String. For example:

```
i = Len("Test ")                          'result: i=5
```

InStr uses this syntax:

```
<integer> = InStr(<string to search>,<string to match>)
```

It searches for <string to match> in <string to search> and returns its position (o = not found). For example:

```
i = Instr("Test ","t")                    'result: i=4
```

Trim uses this syntax:

```
<string> = Trim(<string>)
```

It removes leading and trailing spaces. For example:

```
s = Trim("Test ")                         'result: s="Test"
```

UCase uses this syntax:

```
<string> = UCase(<string>)
```

It returns the uppercase equivalent of the given String. For example:

```
s = UCase("Test ")                        'result: s="TEST "
```

LCase uses this syntax:

```
<string> = LCase(<string>)
```

It returns the lowercase equivalent of the given String. For example:

```
s = LCase("Test ")                              'result: s="test "
```

Left uses this syntax:

```
<string> = Left(<string>,<integer length>)
```

It returns the leftmost <length> characters from a given String. For example:

```
s = Left("Test ",2)                             'result: s="Te"
```

Mid uses this syntax:

```
<string> = Mid(<string>,<integer start pos>,<integer length>)
```

It returns a substring of the specified String, beginning with position <start pos>, for <length> characters. For example:

```
s = Mid("Test ",2,3)                            'result: s="est"
```

Right uses this syntax:

```
<string> = Right(<string>,<integer length>)
```

It returns the rightmost <length> characters from a given String. For example:

```
s = Right("Test ",1)                            'result: s=" "
```

Linking variables to input/output windows

As said, InLines allow you to get the most out of your experiment, but without the ability to interact with your experimental design, they are of limited use. Now that we have some feeling how a variable can be declared and how its content can be manipulated, let's explain how we can actually use it in the experiment. For example, we may want to present some information to the participant who is performing the experiment. Until now, we have used the Debug.Print command to print the content to the output window. However, this screen is only available *after* running the experiment, and can simply not be used to present information to the participant; it is for debugging purposes only.

A very simple alternative is to present information on a screen that pops up in a windows message box, using the **MsgBox** command. The program will then wait until the user clicks *OK* or presses the *ENTER* key. So running the code below:

```
MsgBox "Hello world"
```

results in showing this window during runtime:

Now we can simply show the content of a string, like in this example:

```
Dim s As String
s = "The sum of 3 and 13 is: " & CStr(3+13)
MsgBox s
```

which results in this window:

Instead of showing the content of variables, we can also ask for input from the user. Although this is usually done using response logging in an object, there are situations where you may prefer to use an **InputBox**. This doesn't provide timing information, though. So running this code:

```
Dim NameStr As String
NameStr = InputBox("Your name:","Please enter your name","defaultname")
```

would result in showing this InputBox:

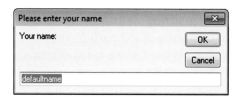

After the user clicked *OK*, the NameStr variable contains the characters entered by the user. While E-Prime® can use the value in this variable during runtime, it will *not* be logged in the edat or text file. To do so, you should use an *attribute*. (How to deal with attributes and reading values from attributes will be discussed in the next section.)

Linking variables to attributes

Although the **MsgBox** and **InputBox** are useful in some cases, it is more common to use variables in combination with *attributes*. That is, we often want to exchange information between your InLine (information stored in *variables*) and your Lists (information stored in *attributes*).

You can *read* the content of attributes using the following syntax:

```
<string name> = c.GetAttrib("<attribute to read>")
```

So, for instance, let's say we have a List that is sequentially presented and we are currently running the third trial:

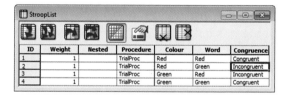

If we run this code

```
Dim s As String
s = c.GetAttrib("Word")
Debug.Print s
```

the output window would show: "Red".

However, it is also possible to read some attributes that are not shown in a List but that are still available in the program. For example, by running the code below, the **Subject** number entered before running the experiment will be printed:

```
Dim s As String
s = c.GetAttrib("Subject")
Debug.Print s
```

Notice that Subject is not an attribute in the List, but because it is a default start-up value of the experiment (see Chapter III), it is automatically made into an attribute. Another example is the attribute **Display.Refreshrate** (this is read only), which is very helpful if you want to check the current refresh rate of the monitor in experiments with critical timing features (e.g. subliminal priming).

So, **c.GetAttrib** reads the actual value of the attribute *depending on the current position in the List*. In other words, it reads the attribute relative to the current *context* (c., for short).

Conversely, we can also set or change particular attributes in the current context. (Note that, in order to store the attribute in a particular List, use the <ListName>. SetAttrib method described in Chapter VII). Assume, for example, that you want to calculate the MeanRT in each trial (as explained earlier) so that the attribute can be presented later in a TextDisplay, using bracket notation. In that case, simply use the c.SetAttrib command, as shown in this example:

```
TrialCounter = TrialCounter + 1
RTSummation = RTSummation + TargetStimulus.RT
Dim MeanRT As Single
MeanRT = (RTSummation / TrialCounter)
c.SetAttrib "MeanRTAttribute", CStr(MeanRT)
```

Note that it is not necessary to add the "MeanRTAttribute" attribute in a List. E-Prime® will simply create it if the attribute it is not found in a List. Moreover, the attribute will be logged in your edat or text file automatically. However, always make sure not to use an *attribute name* that already exists as a *variable name*; their values may unpredictably become mixed up when running your experiment.

So, the syntax to store a value in an attribute is:

```
c.SetAttrib "<Name of the attribute to be saved in>", <string value to save>
```

Notice that this syntax does *not* use round brackets, even though they are necessary for GetAttrib.

▐▌➡ As you may have noticed before, brackets are always necessary when calling a function (which is a subprogram that *returns* a particular value), but they are not allowed when calling a command (which is a subprogram that *does not* return anything). That is why, for example, InputBox() and c.GetAttrib() use brackets; they return a value back to the program. On the other hand, MsgBox and c.SetAttrib don't use brackets because they don't return a value. Syntax is different in other versions of Basic, such as *Visual Basic for Applications*.

Inlines everywhere

InLines are incredibly useful in E-Prime®. Indeed, when we program an experiment in E-Prime®, we seldom use anything but Lists, a few TextDisplays and quite a number of InLines. Let's show some easy and interesting examples of InLine code.

Sleeping and beeping

Well, you could use a Wait object (which has the advantage of response logging), but the following code is the lazy way to achieve the same result:

```
Sleep 2000
```

The **Sleep** command (recall that as this is a command, you don't use brackets) makes your experiment wait for 2000 ms. Its value is of the 'Long' data type, so it must be smaller than 2,147,483,647 (almost 25 days). In order to know when 25 days have elapsed, you may want to set up an alarm. To do this, try:

```
Beep
```

However, note that **Beep** can behave inconsistently; in our old labs (running Windows 98SE and E-Prime 1.2), the beep would only work if the SoundDevice object was *unchecked* or removed entirely from the experiment property (Devices tab). On Michiel's home PC (running Vista x86), it didn't work at all, and more recently, in E-Prime 2, it seems to call a generic Windows sound whether or not the SoundDevice is added. Anyway, you can try this. It's a nice example of what should, in principle, be a very short and simple statement. PST, however, strongly recommends not using it for any time-critical purposes.

Logging Timing

Of course, you might want to do some time auditing without having to run your entire experiment and check the .OnsetDelays and .DurationErrors in the edat or text file. (This is especially true if you are using the Sleep statement mentioned earlier.) Here's the other way of doing it. Let's say you want to log the precision of this sleep statement. For instance:

```
Debug.Print Clock.Read
Sleep 2000
Debug.Print Clock.Read
```

Debug.Print shows you anything you would like to read in the output window (Debug tab) inside E-Prime®. In this case, it shows you whatever the output of **Clock.Read** is. Clock.Read, in turn, returns the current time in milliseconds of E-Prime's clock. It is the time that has elapsed since the beginning of the experiment. So this is "cumulative timing", if you will. When we tried this, the output window showed:

10541
12541

That is, the time before the Sleep statement turned on was 10541 ms, and after it turned off the time was 12541 ms, showing that 2000 ms had elapsed. This is pretty accurate timing, if you consider we are running this under Windows Vista with loads of other programs also running. What happens when E-Prime® does something more interesting than sleeping for 2000 ms? To find out, we inserted a TextDisplay after this InLine, and another small InLine with just "Debug.Print Clock.Read" in it. The TextDisplay is supposed to be shown for 1000 ms. Now, the output shows this:

11211
13211
14223

Notice that:

First, the TextDisplay lasted 1012 ms instead of the 1000 ms that it should have lasted, but this is mostly due to Onset Sync (see Chapter I and Chapter III). Indeed, we tried it again with Onset Sync turned off, and it took 1003 ms, so that's much better. Obviously, it is not actually shown for 1003 ms, though (see Chapter III, on refresh cycles).

Second, the experiment did not start quite at the same time as the previous one: it started about 11211 − 10541 = 670 ms later, actually. This is mainly due to timing errors that occur when you begin data collection directly from the moment the experiment starts running: E-Prime® is still loading some stuff, whilst other, "Windows-governed" processes are still running to some extent. To make sure that the real experiment starts when these processes have finished, always introduce an introduction screen that takes some time to read and that ends by a (unlogged, no correct response) key press.

Ad-hoc randomization

Variables can also be used to read and/or change properties of E-Objects directly. For example, in this chapter, we have used TargetStimulus.RT. This reads the property RT of the E-Object TargetStimulus. It is possible to use InLine in order to alter properties of objects in E-Prime® on the fly. One common property is .Duration. E-Object including Slides, TextDisplays, ImageDisplays and Waits all have a **.Duration property.**

For example, to randomise the duration for **jittering**, you can use the following trick:

Insert a TextDisplay, name it something like Fixation (with a "+" crosshair, for example) on a Procedure. Drag an InLine on the Procedure *before* the TextDisplay. Edit the InLine to something like:

```
Fixation.Duration = Random(10, 2000)
```

Finished! Now, the Fixation's duration is randomised to a length between 10 and 2000 ms. As you may have noticed, there is a major drawback of this quick and dirty randomisation method. In contrast to the nested JitterList approach explained in Chapter III, the draws are more or less random *with replacement*. So, the total duration of the experiment is not entirely predictable. This can be undesirable in certain contexts, for example in fMRI studies that require a fixed duration of the experiment because the MRI scanner uses a fixed number of scans.

Adjusting the speed of your experiment

Another example of a property that can be set by the E-Basic script is **Clock. Scale.** Adjusting this value changes the timing of your experiment accordingly. Although this option is not often used when acquiring data (unless you need some fine-grained adjustments, e.g. to synchronise your processor clock with external hardware), it might be helpful to quickly run through your experiment, say ten times as fast as usual, for debugging purposes. To use this helpful feature, just add an InLine object at the beginning of your experiment with the following line of code:

```
Clock.Scale = 0.1        'Experiment runs 10x faster, debug only!
```

This line of code is only useful when debugging your experiment. Don't forget to remove it, or change it into a comment (so that the compiler will ignore it) as soon as you are ready to bring the experiment to the lab!

E-Prime 2 Professional also includes an *E-Run Test* feature in E-Studio which can speed up the experiment up to a factor of 4.

Tutorial VI: A working memory test

Let's start to program a working memory test (cf. Luck & Vogel, 1997; Sternberg, 1969) that needs some InLine codes to provide feedback to participants about the accuracy of their memory. In this task, we are going to present four letters at arbitrary positions on the screen, which should be recalled after a short time delay. After the participants have entered all the letters they can recall, they will get feedback about which items were recalled correctly.

Step 1: Building the basic design

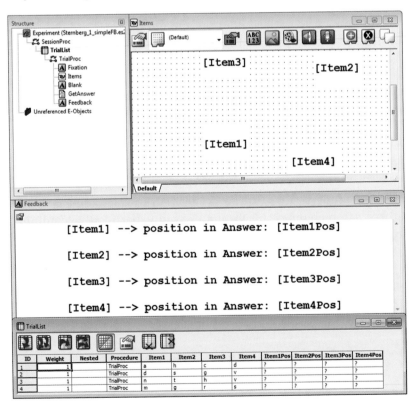

Build the experiment as illustrated in the figure. Set the duration of all objects to 2500 ms. Create a TrialList with 4 levels that are randomly selected (exits after 1 cycle). Add an instruction screen to the beginning of the experiment that explains the goal of this experiment: participants need to memorise all letters presented on the screen, and they are asked to recall as many letters as possible (sequence is arbitrary) a few seconds later.

Step 2: E-Basic coding

We will use the InputBox() function to collect the letters the participant recalls. This function will return the string of characters the participant enters in the InputBox. Note that an InputBox can only be used to measure accuracy. If we had been interested in reaction times, it would have been better to use a recognition task with stimuli being presented sequentially (like in the standard version of the Sternberg working memory task) or to use the advanced properties of response logging (e.g. logging a series of keyboard responses in combination with the so-called **echo** feature). For more information, see the Help file.

The letters recalled by the participants are read into a String using the lines of code shown below. Please add this code to the beginning of your GetAnswer In-Line object:

```
Dim answer As String
answer = InputBox("Try to recall all the letters you just saw ", _
"Your response:")
```

Note that the underscore symbol (_) is used here to break up a line of code so that it is read as a continuous line by the computer despite beginning on a new line.

Don't forget to save the experiment now and to try it out in order to determine whether this part of the experiment runs well.

Since we now know the letters the participants recalled, let's check whether the letters indeed were correctly recalled. In order to test this, we will check whether a given item was part of the participant's response, using the **InStr()** function. As described earlier in this chapter, the *InStr()* function searches a particular String in another String, and returns its position when found. In this tutorial, we will show this position to the participant in the Feedback TextDisplay, using the *Item1Pos* to *Item4Pos* attributes.

So, by using InStr() we want to check for each item (*Item1*, *Item2*, *Item3* and *Item4*) whether it is stored in the *answer* variable, and, if so, the *position* of the item *inside this* variable should be returned. If the item is not found in the *answer* variable, a o (zero) should be returned. In order to log the position and use it in E-Objects, we need to store it in an attribute (*Item1Pos* to store the position of *Item 1*, *Item2Pos* to store the position of *Item 2*, etc.).

The code below does exactly this for *Item 1*:

```
Dim item As String
Dim itempos As Integer
' check whether Item 1 is in the answer, return position and store in attrib
item = c.GetAttrib("Item1")
itempos = InStr(answer, item)
c.SetAttrib "Item1Pos",itempos
```

Add these lines of code to your *GetAnswer* InLine object, and check whether the feedback works correctly for *Item1*.

The next step is obvious: copy the code for *Item 1* and paste them three times. Adapt the code so that *Item2Pos*, *Item3Pos* and *Item4Pos* are also set correctly. So, what we need to add is:

```
' check whether Item 2 is in the answer, return position and store in attrib
item = c.GetAttrib("Item2")
itempos = InStr(answer, item)
c.SetAttrib "Item2Pos",itempos
' check whether Item 3 is in the answer, return position and store in attrib
item = c.GetAttrib("Item3")
itempos = InStr(answer, item)
c.SetAttrib "Item3Pos",itempos
' check whether Item 4 is in the answer, return position and store in attrib
item = c.GetAttrib("Item4")
itempos = InStr(answer, item)
c.SetAttrib "Item4Pos",itempos
```

Run your experiment and check whether the feedback works correctly. Note that the position will be zero when an item was not found to be entered in the Input-Box. We will use this feature to provide colour feedback in the next chapter. For now, that's all folks!

Exercises

- Program a Stroop task that provides feedback about the average accuracy and average reaction time. Use InLine code to provide feedback being presented after each trial using a TextDisplay. Use the example described under the "Math operators" section of this chapter.

- Let's split the experiment into two parts, one for training and one for testing. The training part presents ten trials, and feedback is shown after each trial (like before). In contrast, the testing part consists of four blocks of 20 trials, with a break between blocks. Use a hierarchy of Lists. The List at the top level includes the training block and the testing blocks. Separate subordinate Trial-Lists for the training part and the testing part are needed to run the trials. For the testing trials, feedback about average accuracy and reaction time *during that block only* is presented in the break subsequent to that block.

- Experiment with the Clock.Scale option before and after you have changed the duration of the Stroop stimulus from *infinite* to 1500 ms.

- Use ad hoc randomisation to present a fixation cross for a random duration between 500 and 3000 ms.

Advanced excercises

- Compare the timing information of the response logging with the timing features of Clock.Read in the InLine script run just before and after a stimulus. Use a MsgBox to compare Stimulus.RT with the differences between Clock. Read after versus before the stimulus. Hint: add separate InLines before and after the stimulus that store the value of Clock.Read.

- Use MsgBox and Debug.Print to check the response logging options stored in E-Prime®. For example, check whether it is true that Stimulus.RT equals Stimulus.RTTime – Stimulus.OnsetTime.

- Use a MsgBox that presents the refresh rate of the monitor immediately after starting your experiment. Check whether you can change the monitor settings.

Chapter V

Decision making in E-Basic

In this chapter, you will learn

About: • Decision making in E-Basic using the If-Then statement
• Conditional expressions
• Combining conditional expressions
• Terminating parts of your experiment

How to: • Program an Ultimatum game
• Program a Cyberball game
• Terminate a List of practice trials after a criterion is met
• Provide advanced performance feedback
• Program a break using InLine code

In this chapter you will deal with some more advanced E-Prime® magic. You will learn how to make two very interesting psychological paradigms, namely the Ultimatum and Cyberball games. As these games are based on decision making you need to know how to implement that in your experiments. Therefore, we first explain certain decision structures with the use of flow charts, which greatly helps visualising how one may create a program's decision structure. Also, you will be taught the E-Basic commands, such as If-Then and several important operators (And, Not and the beloved Xor). In addition, you will be shown how to end the whole experiment (or part of it) prematurely (*experimentus interruptus*) based on conditions. In two tutorials this knowledge will be put to use in creating the above mentioned games.

The If-Then statement

Like shopping, programming is all about making the correct decisions. Depending on the actual value of a variable, the computer should run code1, or else it should run code2. That is, depending on the outcome of some comparison, you create some *branching structure* in the program outline.

For example, assume that your critical timing experiment is only allowed to run with a screen refresh rate of 60 Hz. In a flow chart, this is what we would like to do.

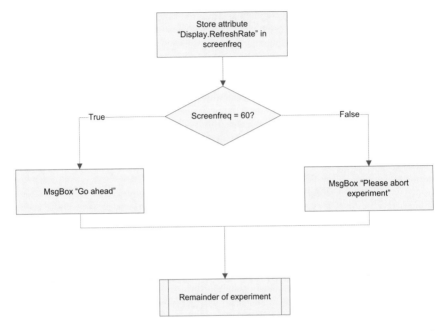

This example demonstrates that we need a control structure (the diamond symbol) that makes a decision: depending on the **conditional expression** (screenfreq = 60) the experiment runs one of the two branches.

To do this in E-Basic, you need the **If-Then-Else-End If statement (short: If-Then statement)**. This combination of statements checks for a set of conditions (if) and does something (then) when the conditional expression is True. Optionally, it does something else (else) when the condition is not met. This is the syntax:

```
If (<conditional expression>) Then
    '<does something, put these lines of code here>
    '<line 1>
    '<line 2>
    '<Etc...>
Else
    '<does something else, put these lines of code here >
    '<line 1>
    '<line 2>
    '<Etc...>
End If
```

▐▌➡ We strongly recommend you use the indentation shown in this syntax example. Either use four spaces or a tab. However, indentation is generally only there for clarity: E-Basic compilers and interpreters rarely care how much whitespace is present in-between programming statements.

As an example, let's assume that we want to check whether the screen refresh rate is 60 Hz (in reality it is more likely not to be an integer value), and show the result in a Msgbox. From the last chapter we learned to use the *Display.RefreshRate* attribute to retrieve this information. Because we want to compare this value in decimal precision, we first convert it to a Single, using the CSng command. Now we can compare the value in *Display,RefreshRate* with the value 60. The corresponding code may look like this:

```
Dim screenfreq As Single
screenfreq = CSng(C.GetAttrib("Display.RefreshRate"))
If (screenfreq = 60) Then
    MsgBox "Go ahead. The refresh rate is fine"
Else
    MsgBox "Please abort the experiment. The refresh rate is " _
        & C.GetAttrib("Display.RefreshRate")
End If
```

Or, after some code substitution, we will get:

```
If (CSng(C.GetAttrib("Display.RefreshRate")) = 60) Then
    MsgBox "Go ahead. The refresh rate is fine"
Else
    MsgBox "Please abort the experiment. The refresh rate is " _
      & C.GetAttrib("Display.RefreshRate")
End If
```

Combining conditional expressions

Now, let's assume we would like to combine criteria in the conditional expression. For instance, we can also check whether we run the experiment for piloting purposes only, where timing is not critical (i.e. in cases where no data was logged because the experimenter used subject number 0), or for data acquisition in the lab, where timing is absolutely critical (the subject number is greater than 0). We might then decide to do the refresh rate check only if *subject number > 0*.

There are at least two possible implementations for this solution.

Solution 1: Use nested If-Then structures

We can nest the If-Then structure within another If-Then structure. The flow chart shows how this may look:

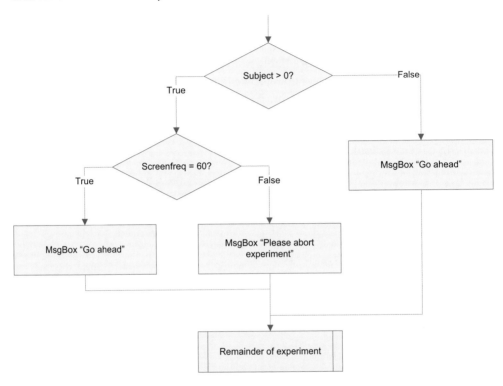

This will translate into the following E-Basic code:

```
If (CInt(C.GetAttrib("Subject")) > 0) Then
    If (CSng(C.GetAttrib("Display.RefreshRate")) = 60) Then
        MsgBox "Go ahead. The refresh rate is fine"
    Else
        MsgBox "Please abort the experiment. The refresh rate is " _
            & C.GetAttrib("Display.RefreshRate")
    End If
Else
    MsgBox "Go ahead. The refresh rate is fine"
End If
```

Although the code looks quite complicated, the indentation is of great help in understanding the nested structure. The second solution, however, is much simpler.

Solution 2: combine conditional expressions

We can combine conditional expressions using something called **logical operators**, such as **And** (returns True if both expressions are True), **Or** (returns True if either expression is True), **Not** (returns True if expression is False, and returns False if expression is True), and **Xor** (returns True if only one expression is True). The behaviour of these standard logical operators can be described in **truth tables**, which you may remember from high school.

For example, the Or operator only returns True if at least one of the two conditional expressions is True. In our case, the 'Go ahead' message should be presented when Subject = 0 *Or* when Display.RefreshRate = 60. Otherwise, the 'Please abort' Msgbox should be presented.

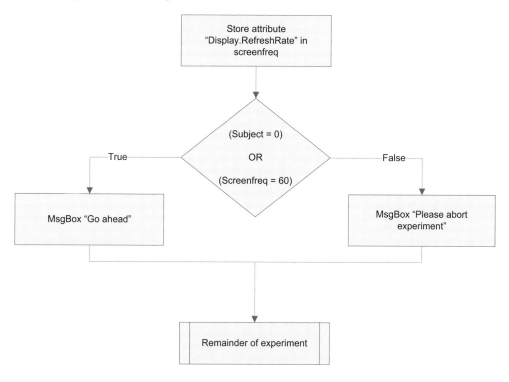

To temporarily store the value of a conditional expression you can use a *Boolean* variable (this data type only stores the values True or False). This would look like:

```
Dim b As Boolean
b = ((CInt(C.GetAttrib("Subject")) = 0) Or _
  (CSng(C.GetAttrib("Display.RefreshRate")) = 60)
If (b) Then
    'subject = 0 Or Refreshrate = 60
    MsgBox "Go ahead. The refresh rate is fine"
Else
    MsgBox "Please abort the experiment. The refresh rate is " _
      & C.GetAttrib("Display.RefreshRate")
End If
```

Although the Boolean variable may improve the readability of your script, it is not absolutely necessary. After some substitution, we got rid of the variable:

```
If ((CInt(C.GetAttrib("Subject")) = 0) Or _
(CSng(C.GetAttrib("Display.RefreshRate")) = 60) Then
    'subject = 0 Or Refreshrate = 60
    MsgBox "Go ahead. The refresh rate is fine"
Else
    MsgBox "Please abort the experiment. The refresh rate is " _
      & C.GetAttrib("Display.RefreshRate")
End If
```

Comparing values

When using conditional expressions, you can use all sorts of standard **comparison operators**, such as < (less than), > (greater than), = (equal to), >= (greater than or equal to), <= (less than or equal to), and <> (not equal to).

Some examples of these comparisons are shown below. For demonstration purposes, we store the result of the conditional expression in the Boolean variable b.

```
Dim b As Boolean
b = (3 > 5)      'result: b = False
b = (3 <= 3)     'result: b = True
b = (3 <> 4)     'result: b = True
b = (2 < 3)      'result: b = True
```

The funny thing is that these mathematical expressions may also be used to compare single characters. In that case, the standard alphabet is used as the order criterion with capital letters listed before the lower-case letters, as in this sequence ABC...XYZabc....xyz. See the examples below.

```
Dim b As Boolean
b = ("a" > "d")          'result: b = False
b = ("Z" <= "a")         'result: b = True
b = ("a" <> "A")         'result: b = True
b = ("A" < "C")          'result: b = True
```

How to terminate parts of your experiment

Until now, we have mostly brought up a key-combination (*ctrl+alt+shift*) to abort experiments. However, it is also possible to create an *experimentus interruptus* using a line of E-Basic code. There are several ways you can do this.

Solution 1: Skip the remainder of the experiment

Skipping the remainder of the experiment by jumping to the end of the experiment is an elegant solution to abort your experiment. You simply add a *GoTo statement* in the script that describes the Label to jump to. So add a **Label** (see Chapter III) to the end of your session Procedure and use the GoTo statement in the script. Using the *refresh rate check* example again, the following code will jump to the Label EndOfExperiment if the refresh rate doesn't equal 60.

```
If (CSng(C.GetAttrib("Display.RefreshRate")) = 60) Then
   MsgBox "Go ahead. The refresh rate is fine"
Else
   MsgBox "THE EXPERIMENT WILL BE ABORTED! The refresh rate is " _
     & C.GetAttrib("Display.RefreshRate")
   GoTo EndOfExperiment          'Jumps to the end of the experiment
End If
```

These lines of code were used in the CheckRefreshRate InLine object in the experimental Procedure shown below. Note the EndOfExperiment Label flags the end of the session Procedure. Although the Label solution is elegant, it is of limited use because it is only possible to jump to a Label *within the same Procedure*.

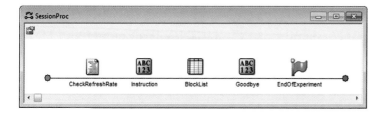

Solution 2: Abort the Procedure that is running

It is also possible to abort the Procedure that is currently running. You simply use the three-letter command **End.**

```
If (CSng(C.GetAttrib("Display.RefreshRate")) = 60) Then
   MsgBox "Go ahead. The refresh rate is fine"
Else
   MsgBox "THE EXPERIMENT WILL BE ABORTED! The refresh rate is " _
      & C.GetAttrib("Display.RefreshRate")
   End  'Crude method to abort procedure
End If
```

However, this is a crude method and problems with data logging are likely to occur. Moreover, the command only aborts the Procedure that is currently running. Consequently, the End command will only stop the entire experiment when it is called from an InLine located in a SessionProc.

As the use of End usually induces data logging problems our advice is to use it only when you are sure you are never going to analyse the data the experiment produces. In many circumstances it might therefore be better to use a variant of the solution that is described next.

Solution 3: Terminate the List that is running

Imagine you would like to run a List of practice trials until a particular criterion is met. In that case you may want to terminate the current List that is running using the **<ListName>.Terminate** command.

For example, the code below will terminate a PracTrialList if at least 11 trials have passed AND the average accuracy is 80% or higher.

```
If ((TrialCounter > 10) And (MeanACC >= 0.8)) Then
   PracTrialList.Terminate
End If
```

Note that this script simply assumes that the variables TrialCounter and Mean-ACC contain the correct values. The previous chapter has already explained how to perform these calculations.

Solution 4: Combine the End and Terminate statements

If you would like to abort your experiment while you are in the middle of running a List, which is embedded in another List itself, you should call the Terminate command first for all relevant Lists, before you call the 'dangerous' *End* command.

In the example below, we would like to stop the entire experiment in the Check In-Line object. In this case, we simply need to call the Terminate commands for the TrialList and the main BlockList. After that we use the End statement to prevent the Stim2 from being shown to the user.

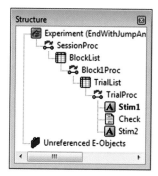

So, we need at least the following lines of codes:

```
TrialList.Terminate
BlockList.Terminate
End
```

However, given the use of the End command, problems are likely to be anticipated, so don't use it if possible. Perhaps it is better to add an EndOfTrial Label at the end of the TrialProc and use this code instead

```
TrialList.Terminate
BlockList.Terminate
GoTo EndOfTrial
```

Tutorial VII: The Ultimatum game

Assume you receive 10 euros to be divided between you and another person. You (the allocator) can propose a particular division and the other person (the recipient) can either accept or reject the proposed division. If the recipient accepts your offer, then the money is divided as proposed. If the recipient rejects, however, both will receive nothing. What kind of division would you propose? Usually you may suggest a fair offer because chances are higher that this offer will not be rejected. However, this decision may depend on several factors. The Ultimatum game can be used to investigate this question in an experimental way (Güth, Schmittberger & Schwarze, 1982).

In this tutorial, we are going to program an Ultimatum game where the allocator can either decide to propose a fair offer (5 points for me, 5 points for you) or an unfair offer (7 points for me, 3 points for you). After the participant makes the decision, feedback about the recipient's response is shown on the screen. You invent a cover story in the description: e.g. tell that the recipient is a real person connected to your experiment via internet. In reality, the recipient is a virtual agent and just consists of some lines of E-Basic code that makes decisions in a human-like rational way with some random variation. Let's assume that the following algorithm determines the behaviour of the artificial recipients:

When a fair offer is proposed by the allocator, I will accept it 80% of the time;
when an unfair offer is proposed by the allocator, I will accept it only 25% of the time.

Step 1: Building the basic design

After an instruction screen, we present this TrialList:

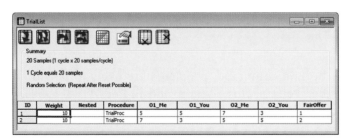

Note that O1 and O2 stand for Offer1 and Offer2, respectively.

The TrialProc consist of the following objects:

The DecisionMe should present two offers and waits until the user decides to press either the numerical key *1* or the numerical key *2*. Note that we don't have a normative 'correct response' available here, although there is certainly a fair response (as indicated in the List). So, leave the CorrectResponse field empty.

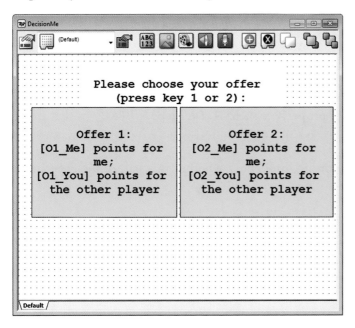

In order to mark the offer just selected by the participant, we will show a red border around the offer selected. First draw these borders in the FeedbackMe SlideObject (Use SlideTexts and change the BorderColor and BorderWidth properties). Make sure that the background of all (sub)objects has been set to *transparent* and that two Slide states are available: 'Resp1' and 'Resp2'. Set the duration to 1000 ms.

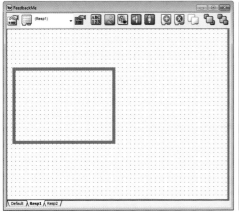 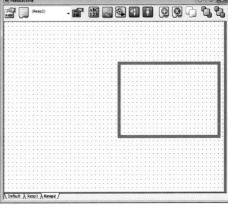

Okay, let's now define the code needed to set the SlideObject feedback in the SetFeedbackMe InLine object. The following lines change the ActiveState of the object, depending on the response given in the DecisionMe object.

```
If DecisionMe.RESP = "1" Then
    FeedbackMe.ActiveState = "Resp1"
Else
    FeedbackMe.ActiveState = "Resp2"
End If
```

⫸ A more efficient way to achieve the same end result would be to set the FeedbackMe's ActiveState property to *"RESP"[DecisionMe.RESP]*. In that case, you don't need the SetFeedbackMe InLine object. Check it out!

Before continuing programming, first check whether this part of the experiment runs correctly.

Now let's change the layout of the WaitingForOther Slide object. Make the background transparent and use a fixed duration of say 4500 ms.

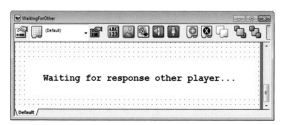

Also add the the DecisionOther Slide. Use two transparent Slidestates as shown below. Again, set duration to 4500 ms.

Step 2: Program the behaviour of the recipient

The most important part should be done now: we will add some artificial intelligence to the experiment that determines the recipient's decision and change the DecisionOther.ActiveState accordingly.

First, let's determine whether the offer was fair or not, and store this in the *variable* ChoiceIsFair as well as in the *attribute* ChoiceWasFair (so that this attribute is stored in the edat file to be analysed later).

```
'first determine whether offer chosen was fair or unfair
Dim ChoiceIsFair As Boolean
If DecisionMe.Resp = "1" And C.GetAttrib("FairOffer") = "1" Then
    ChoiceIsFair = True
End If
If DecisionMe.Resp = "1" And C.GetAttrib("FairOffer") = "2" Then
    ChoiceIsFair = False
End If
If DecisionMe.Resp = "2" And C.GetAttrib("FairOffer") = "1" Then
    ChoiceIsFair = False
End If
If DecisionMe.Resp = "2" And C.GetAttrib("FairOffer") = "2" Then
    ChoiceIsFair = True
End If
C.SetAttrib "ChoiceWasFair", ChoiceIsFair
```

This should work. Note that the Else part in the If-Then-Else-End If statement is omitted, because we did not need it here. This is not problematic given that the Else-part is *optional* anyway.

The code just presented uses four successive If-Then statements; however, a closer look reveals that it is much simpler to directly compare the DecisionMe.Resp value with the C.GetAttrib('FairOffer') value. This would result in these lines of code:

```
'first determine whether offer chosen was fair or unfair
Dim ChoiceIsFair As Boolean
If (DecisionMe.Resp = C.GetAttrib("FairOffer")) Then
    ChoiceIsFair = True
Else
    ChoiceIsFair = False
End If
C.SetAttrib "ChoiceWasFair", ChoiceIsFair
```

That's much easier to read, right? And this block of code does exactly the same job!

However, you may recognise that the If-Then statement is in fact completely redundant. So, we can simply store the conditional expression in the Boolean variable directly:

```
'first determine whether offer chosen was fair or unfair
Dim ChoiceIsFair As Boolean
ChoiceIsFair = (DecisionMe.Resp = C.GetAttrib("FairOffer"))
C.SetAttrib "ChoiceWasFair", ChoiceIsFair
```

The second line of this code also nicely demonstrates the two different functions the **= operator** can have in E-Basic. The first = operator is used for *assignment*, whereas the second = operator is used for a *comparison*. It is both elegant and confusing at the same time. Indeed, other programming languages often use different operators for assignment and comparison.

Whichever solution you prefer, after implementing one of the three blocks of codes, we now know whether the allocator provided a fair or an unfair offer.

The next step is to add the intelligence to our artificial recipient. Recall that we decided to use the following rule: when a fair offer is proposed by the allocator, the recipient will accept it 80% of the time; when an unfair offer is proposed by the allocator, the recipient will accept it only 25% of the time.

So there is some randomness in the recipient's behaviour. We'll assume, then, that the recipient draws a random number between 1 and 100 first, which will be used to add the random variation to the decision.

```
'first draw a random number
Dim rnum As Integer
rnum = random(1,100)
```

Now, let's first draw a flowchart depicting the actual algorithm we need (see next page):

So, we need some nested If-Then statements that set the value of whether the recipient accepts or doesn't accept the offer. Store that value in the Boolean variable *OtherAccepts*. At the end of the decision structure, we set the ActiveState property of the Slide DecisionOther accordingly.

This is the code you need:

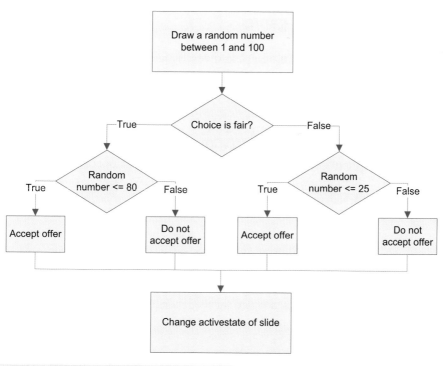

```
Dim OtherAccepts As Boolean
'Now decide what to do
If ChoiceIsFair = True Then
    'Fair in 80% of the cases accept
    If rnum <= 80 Then
        OtherAccepts = True
    Else
        OtherAccepts = False
    End If

Else
    'In 25% of the cases accept
    If rnum <= 25 Then
        OtherAccepts = True
    Else
        OtherAccepts = False
    End If

End If
'Set the Activestate
If OtherAccepts Then
    DecisionOther.ActiveState = "AcceptOffer"
Else
    DecisionOther.ActiveState = "RejectOffer"
End If
```

Now check whether the program works correctly. Are you indeed inclined to give more fair than unfair responses?

Tutorial VIII: The Cyberball game

The Cyberball game allows psychologists to investigate the effects of social exclusion (ostracism). Dr Kipling D. Williams came up with this idea after a Frisbee rolled up and hit him in the back when relaxing in a park in 1983:

> He turned around, saw two other guys looking at him expectantly, and threw the Frisbee back to them. He was a bit surprised when they threw the disk back to him; he walked toward them to form a triangle, and threw it back again. For about a minute, the three of them threw the Frisbee around in a spirited game of catch. What happened next sparked an idea as to how to study the effects of ostracism. For no apparent reason, the two original players started throwing the Frisbee only to each other, and never threw it to the newcomer again. After sheepishly back-stepping toward his dog, the author was amazed at how bad he felt. He was sad, embarrassed, and a bit angry. He wondered what he had done to warrant being ostracised by the other two players. He sought comfort from his faithful dog. Then, it occurred to him that something like this, adapted for the laboratory, would be an excellent means to study ostracism and social exclusion. (Williams & Jarvis, 2006, p.174).

This is the instruction participants usually receive:

> Welcome to Cyberball, the Interactive Ball-Tossing Game Used for Mental Visualisation!
>
> In the upcoming experiment, we test the effects of practising mental visualisation on task performance. Thus, we need you to practise your mental visualisation skills. We have found that the best way to do this is to have you play an on-line ball tossing game with other participants who are logged on at the same time.
>
> In a few moments, you will be playing a ball tossing game with other students over our network. The game is very simple. When the ball is tossed to you, simply use the keyboard to indicate the player (with numerical key 1 or 3) you want to throw it to. When the game is over, the experimenter will give you additional instructions.
>
> What is important is not your ball tossing performance, but that you MENTALLY VISUALISE the entire experience. Imagine what the others look like. What sort of people are they? Where are you playing? Is it warm and sunny or cold and rainy? Create in your mind a complete mental picture of what might be going on if you were playing this game in real life.
>
> Okay, ready to begin?

And this is what the game looks like at the start:

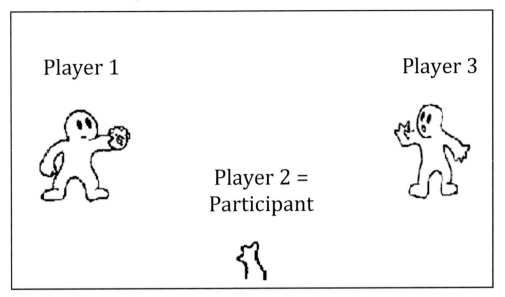

Step 1: Programming the basic experimental flow

How to program the game? Well, first you need some movies that show a ball moving between the players. You need six of them depicting all possible directions:

From player 1 to player 2	(1to2.wmv)
From player 1 to player 3	(1to3.wmv)
From player 2 to player 1	(2to1.wmv)
From player 2 to player 3	(2to3.wmv)
From player 3 to player 1	(3to1.wmv)
From player 3 to player 2	(3to2.wmv)

The six movie files can be downloaded from www.e-primer.com. Please make sure that these movie files are stored in the same folder as your E-Prime® experiment! Note that these small Windows Media Files were converted from the original animated gifs freely available on K.D. Willams' website: www1.psych.purdue.edu/~willia55/Announce/cyberball.htm.

Now let's draw the basic flowchart for each trial, which determines which movies should be played when:

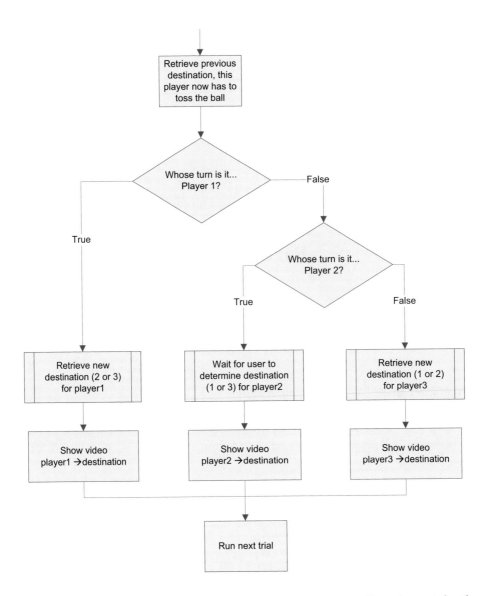

This flowchart basically decides who is throwing the ball in this trial (Player 1, Player 2, or Player 3) and, using attribute retrieval from Lists (see next step), it will decide the destination of the ball.

At any moment throughout the experiment we need to have access to which player is currently playing the ball. So, create a global variable (in the *User Script*) of the Integer type and name it 'CurrentPlayer'.

```
Dim CurrentPlayer As Integer
```

Give this variable the initial value 1, *at the beginning of your SessionProc* (the game always starts with Player 1 throwing the ball). As shown here:

```
CurrentPlayer = 1
```

Okay, now implement the basic branching structure. Depending on the value in CurrentPlayer, the script may run one single trial in either ListPlayer1, ListPlayer2, or ListPlayer3. In order to do so, we make use of a combination of Lists and Labels in a TrialProc. Build a basic setup running 60 trials, as in the example below:

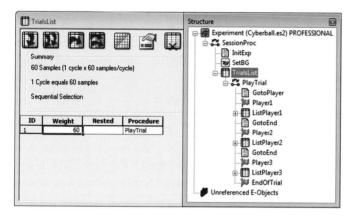

The actual branching is done by the GotoPlayer InLine script:

```
If CurrentPlayer = 1 Then
    GoTo Player1
Else
    If CurrentPlayer = 2 Then
        GoTo Player2
    Else
        GoTo Player3
    End If
End If
```

And the GotoEnd Inline scripts jump to the EndOfTrial label:

```
GoTo EndOfTrial
```

Note: Although you can implement all possible ways of branching using nested If-Then statements. E-Basic also allows for complicated branching structures using the **ElseIf** statement and the **Select...Case** statement. Please refer to the E-Basic help file for more information.

Step 2: Programming the behavior of Player 1 and Player 3

Let's now consider how to set up the ListPlayer1 and ListPlayer3. These Lists should retrieve the new destination the virtual Players 1 and 3 will use to toss the ball to. So add an attribute called 'TargetPlayer' and type in the possible destinations of that player (a player is not allowed to toss the ball to himself; it would be a cool extension of the paradigm though). These Lists completely determine the behaviour of Player 1 and Player 3. Depending on your interest you can make this behaviour for example predictable (use sequential selection), random (use random selection), or preferential (increase the weight of one of the TargetPlayers).

Important: because each player is only allowed to toss the ball *once in a row*, please make sure both Lists *exit* after *one sample*! Don't change the *reset sampling* settings. Make sure you understand the difference.

The example below implements a very predictable and non-preferential playing style for both players.

Play1Proc and *Play3Proc* consist of an InLine script (name it 'PreparePlayer1' and 'PreparePlayer3') and a subsequently presented MovieDisplay (name is always 'PlayerMovieDisplay1'). In this MovieDisplay, specify a (temporary) filename (e.g. use '1to2.wmv'), use the Stretch function, change the frame dimensions to 50% x 50%, and use a black border colour (width 4). In addition, set the *Duration* to *infinite*, do *not* specify Start and Stop position (the movie will be shown completely) and set *End Movie Action* to *Terminate*.

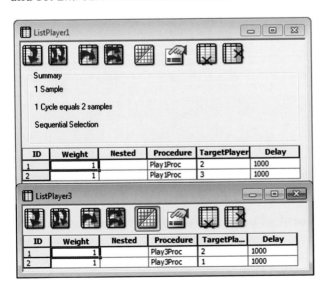

ListPlayer1

Summary
1 Sample
1 Cycle equals 2 samples
Sequential Selection

ID	Weight	Nested	Procedure	TargetPlayer	Delay
1	1		Play1Proc	2	1000
2	1		Play1Proc	3	1000

ListPlayer3

ID	Weight	Nested	Procedure	TargetPla...	Delay
1	1		Play3Proc	2	1000
2	1		Play3Proc	1	1000

Now, add this code in PreparePlayer1:

```
PlayerMovieDisplay1.FileName = "1to" & C.GetAttrib("TargetPlayer")&".wmv"
CurrentPlayer = C.GetAttrib("TargetPlayer")
```

This script overwrites the temporary filename in the MovieDisplay with the correct filename. The second line is also very important. Here, the value of the variable CurrentPlayer is updated to the new destination, so that in the next trial the branching structure knows who has become the CurrentPlayer.

Almost the same code should be added to the PreparePlayer3 InLine:

```
PlayerMovieDisplay1.FileName = "3to" & C.GetAttrib("TargetPlayer")&".wmv"
CurrentPlayer = C.GetAttrib("TargetPlayer")
```

Now, we are almost ready to start the experiment. The only thing missing is the definition of Player 2, the active participant.

Step 3: Programming Player 2

First, add a Procedure named 'Play2Proc' to the ListPlayer2. We don't need any attribute in this List. Again, make sure the List *exits* after one sample.

Do the same for Play2Proc, as you did for Play1Proc and Play3Proc: add an InLine script (name it 'PreparePlayer2') and a subsequently presented PlayerMovieDisplay1. Now add a Wait object to the *beginning of the Procedure* (name it 'WaitForUserResponse') and let it log the responses 1 and 3. The Wait object has infinite duration and it will be terminated as soon as the user has decided which player (s)he wants to toss the ball to (i.e. Player 1 or 3).

Now, to show the correct movie after the response to the WaitForUserResponse object, we need the following code in the PreparePlayer2 script:

```
PlayerMovieDisplay1.FileName = "2to" & WaitForUserResponse.RESP &".wmv"
CurrentPlayer = WaitForUserResponse.RESP
```

Done! Compare the structure of your experiment with the flowchart. Were all steps implemented correctly? You should now be able to play your first game created in E-Prime® Enjoy!

Exercises

- Adapt the Stroop task you have implemented during the exercise in Chapter IV. Terminate the training List after *at least* ten trials have passed AND the average accuracy > 90%. See the example about the *<ListName>.Terminate* command described in this chapter.

- The FeedbackDisplay is a Slide Display that includes some built-in decision making about which response is given, and whether the response was correct or not. Implement a Slide Display that will have the same functionality as the FeedbackDisplay by using InLine code to determine its ActiveState. So, the InLine code should decide whether the State Correct, Incorrect, or No Response is activated. Add a Stimulus display in which the responses are logged, and check whether your script works correctly.

- Add an extra state to the Slide Display that will become active when you make very fast responses (RT < 100 ms).

- Open the Working Memory task you created in Tutorial VI (Chapter IV). However, instead of the TextDisplay, use a Slide object that resembles the Items Slide layout except that it now provides colour feedback about the correctly recalled Items. Items that were recalled correctly should get a ForeColour of Green, whereas items not recalled should get a ForeColour of Red. Use attributes that determine the ForeColour of the items in the feedback Slide. Set the attributes in the GetAnswer script, using something that looks like this:

```
If itempos <> 0 Then
    c.SetAttrib "Item1FB", "Green"
Else
    c.SetAttrib "Item1FB", "Red"
End If
```

Advanced exercises

Trials are usually presented in blocks after a short break is introduced. To program blocks of trials, you may use a hierarchy of Lists. One List defines the number of blocks, which runs BlockProcs. Within the individual BlockProcs, you can define TrialLists that exit after the number of trials in that blocks have run.

In this additional exercise we will explain an alternative to the hierarchy of List solution, using E-Basic.

Start by adding a text display just prior to a fixation screen. Ask your participant whether he/she wants to continue to the next trial, and press an (allowable!) key to continue.

If the participant doesn't want to continue to the next trial, they are taking a break – which you can of course keep track of by looking at the reaction time of this object (providing you log it), so you would know if they are having too many breaks. The problem, however, is not that the participants take too much time breaking or being 'lazy'. On the contrary, in our experience with reaction time experiments, we found that they are usually very eager to 'get it done with'. Such insights have prompted us to specify *when* they are pausing and *how long* exactly. Should you have 200 trials, it makes sense to let the participant have a break after 100 trials.

Thus, our goal is to hide the pause-screen during the other 199 trials.

First, you need to keep track of the trial number, so make a global variable and call it something like 'TrialCounter'. As you know, global (accessible throughout your experiment) variables are defined in the User part of the script. Enter the following code:

```
Dim TrialCounter as Integer
```

Don't forget to give TrialCounter the initial value 0, somewhere at the beginning of your SessionProc.

During each trial, we want TrialCounter to go up by 1, so in trial one, TrialCounter is also equal to 1 (this may sound like common knowledge, but in programming, 'the first' is often the 0-value). Thus, insert an InLine object at the very beginning of the trial, and write the following statement:

```
TrialCounter = TrialCounter + 1
```

Now, edit your last InLine-object (the TrialCounter = TrialCounter + 1) so it *basically* says:

```
If TrialCounter Is_Not <trial-when-you-want-a-break> Then
    GoTo <whatever you named that label>.
End If
```

Note that Is_Not is not a proper operator, so use the <>-operator instead.

Run your experiment and check whether you see the pause-display

Chapter VI

Loops and Arrays in E-Basic

In this chapter, you will learn

About: • Loops
• Arrays and how to combine them with Lists
• User-defined data types

How to: • Use quasi-random trial selection
• Program a working memory task with different load conditions

The most important thing you will learn in this chapter is how to make quasi-randomised Lists and implement that knowledge into a working memory task. Unfortunately, creating such Lists is not that straightforward. You will need In-Line scripts to put stimuli in your own List (called an **Array**), shuffle that Array, check it, determine if it is shuffled according to specific criteria of your choice and put your shuffled Array back into the List of the experiment. We will start by highlighting the various programming elements – basically, loops and Arrays – that are needed to fulfil this task and continue to explain the specific quasi randomisation method (which also appears on the E-Prime® Support page) in detail.

Looping with Labels

Until now, we have learned to use variables, If-Then statements, and Labels. These are the basic elements of E-Basic, which allow you to implement almost any code you need. Assume, for instance, that you would like to present the numbers 1 to 10 in ten message boxes presented in a row. You now know that these lines of code should simply work:

```
MsgBox "1"
MsgBox "2"
MsgBox "3"
MsgBox "4"
MsgBox "5"
MsgBox "6"
MsgBox "7"
MsgBox "8"
MsgBox "9"
MsgBox "10"
```

However, imagine that you need 100 of these boxes. The trouble is that we would have a severe case of *Repetitive Strain Injury* for writing out all this code. Fortunately there is an easy solution. Given that we know how to use variables, the implementation below is much more flexible, and doesn't need that much code:

```
Dim Counter As Integer
Counter = 1
START_OF_LOOP:
    MsgBox CStr(Counter)
    Counter = Counter + 1
If Counter <= 10 Then
    GoTo START_OF_LOOP
End If
```

The code above implements a structure that is known as a simple **loop**. Here, this loop repeats the MsgBox line of code ten times, with values in Counter increasing from 1 to 10 with each repetition. Note that the START_OF_LOOP line (with the colon!) marks a particular location in the script with a Label. This is the textual equivalent of the Label object that can be dragged into your experimental timeline (as explained in Chapter III).

The flowchart on the next page shows the corresponding function. Note that the arrow pointing upwards loops back to the previous location in the code marked by the Label.

However, given that we still need eight lines of code, the smart guys once developing BASIC decided to add some extra looping structures that need even fewer lines of code.

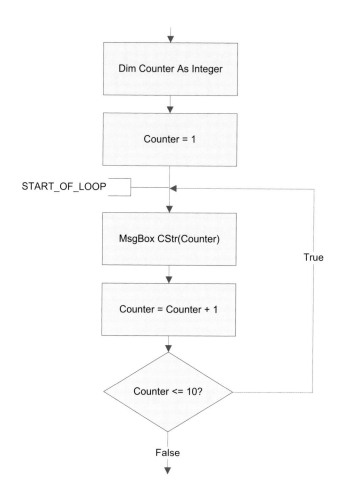

The For-Next Loop

The **For-Next loop** has been invented to repeat some lines of code for a number of times. This is the syntax you need:

```
For <NumberVar> = <LowerRange> To <UpperRange>
    '<Lines of codes to be repeated>
Next
```

Basically, a For-Next loop repeats all code between two markers, the beginning (*For*) marker and the end (*Next*) marker. The two numbers for LowerRange and UpperRange will then be used to establish a consecutive loop for all whole numbers between and including these numbers. The code in between will be executed for each number individually.

The code below shows how a For-Next loop can be used to show the ten message boxes from the previous example (showing the numbers 1,2,3,4,5,6,7,8,9,10, respectively).

```
Dim Counter As Integer
For Counter = 1 To 10
    MsgBox CStr(Counter)
Next
```

This is only four lines of code, rather than the ten or eight lines from the previous section! Moreover, the structure is extremely flexible: you only need to change the values 1 and 10 into the range of values you prefer and the loop will run through it.

Now, let's apply our knowledge to change the repetitive code programmed during the Working Memory tutorial VI (in Chapter IV). The code below shows the repetitive character, with the information that is varied printed in bold font:

```
'check whether Item 1 is in the answer
item = c.GetAttrib("Item1")
itempos = InStr(answer, item)
c.SetAttrib "Item1Pos",itempos
'check whether Item 2 is in the answer
item = c.GetAttrib("Item2")
itempos = InStr(answer, item)
c.SetAttrib "Item2Pos",itempos
'check whether Item 3 is in the answer
item = c.GetAttrib("Item3")
itempos = InStr(answer, item)
c.SetAttrib "Item3Pos",itempos
'check whether Item 4 is in the answer
item = c.GetAttrib("Item4")
itempos = InStr(answer, item)
c.SetAttrib "Item4Pos",itempos
```

To make this code much easier to read, we now replace the bold information with a counter variable x integrated in a For-Next loop. Variable x loops through the numbers 1 to 4. Note that the values from x are referred to in the lines of code that are repeated, like this:

```
Dim x As Integer
For x = 1 To 4
    'check whether Item x is in the answer
    item = c.GetAttrib("Item" & CStr(x))
    itempos = InStr(answer, item)
    c.SetAttrib "Item" & CStr(x) & "Pos",itempos
Next
```

One additional advantage of this implementation is that the code now allows us to extend our Working Memory task much more easily. For instance, imagine a version of the experiment in which you vary the working memory load (number of items presented) per trial. In that case, the number of items that need to be checked depends on the trial that is currently running. To implement this we simply replace the value 4 with a variable that determines the working memory load. In the example below we assume that this value can be retrieved from an attribute called 'NumberOfItems'.

```
Dim x As Integer
Dim wmload As Integer
wmload = c.GetAttrib("NumberOfItems")
For x = 1 To wmload
    'check whether Item x is in the answer
    item = c.GetAttrib("Item" & CStr(x))
    itempos = InStr(answer, item)
    c.SetAttrib "Item" & CStr(x) & "Pos",itempos
Next
```

We hope this example convinces you that the For-Next loop is a very helpful statement to use when you need to flexibly repeat particular lines of code.

As you have learned throughout this book, the majority of repetitions in an experiment need not be programmed manually. List objects are usually of great help in handling most repetitions of Procedures and InLines and loops are usually not needed in those situations.

Loops with conditional expressions

A second type of structure that often is very useful in programming is a loop with a conditional expression. In this type of structure a conditional expression determines the number of loops.

Imagine that you would like to create a casino game where you throw a dice until you get '6'. In E-Basic terms, you would like to draw a random number between 1 and 6 until the conditional expression (random_number = 6) is true. All draws, separated by semicolons, are repetitively shown in a MsgBox.

To do this, you need these lines of code:

```
Dim randnum As Integer
Dim s As String
s = ""
'Below is the casino game loop
Do
    randnum = Random(1,6)            'draw a random number between 1 and 6
    s = s & ";" & CStr(randnum)      'add random number to s
    MsgBox s
Loop Until (randnum = 6)
```

Here the loop continues to run *until* the conditional expression becomes True. Obviously, because the conditional expression depends on a random number, the number of loops is not fixed in this case.

The **Do – Loop Until** structure in the example loops at least one time. This is the syntax:

```
Do
    'lines of codes to be repeated
Loop Until (<conditional_expression>)
```

Now, imagine that we would like to check the conditional expression *before* entering the loop. In that case we need to insert the Until... part immediately after the initial Do statement. As a result, this **Do Until – Loop** structure loops zero or more times.

```
Do Until (<conditional_expression>)
    'lines of codes to be repeated
Loop
```

Imagine you would like to play the casino game only if you did not get the number 6 in a first round. In that case, you will need to check the conditional expression first before you decide whether you would like to run the loop anyway. Here is how you may implement this adapted game:

```
Dim randnum As Integer
Dim s As String
s = ""
'First round: draw a random number
randnum = Random(1,6)   'draw a random number between 1 and 6
'Below is the casino game loop
Do Until (randnum = 6)
    randnum = Random(1,6)            'draw a random number between 1 and 6
    s = s & ";" & CStr(randnum)      'add random number to s
    MsgBox s
Loop
```

Instead of using the **Until** statement, you could also have used the **While** statement. Which one you choose is simply a matter of phrasing or personal preference. As you will see below, using the *While* statement instead of the *Until* statement simply requires you to adapt the phrasing of the conditional expression.

So, this is the syntax of the **Do – Loop While** structure:

```
Do
    'lines of codes to be repeated
Loop While (<conditional_expression>)
```

And this is the syntax of the **Do While – Loop** structure:

```
Do While (<conditional_expression>)
    'lines of codes to be repeated
Loop
```

The example below shows an implementation of the original casino game using a Do – Loop While structure instead of the Do – Loop Until structure:

```
Dim randnum As Integer
Dim s As String
s = ""
'Below is the casino game loop
Do
    randnum = Random(1,6)          'draw a random number between 1 and 6
    s = s & ";" & CStr(randnum)    'add random number to s
    MsgBox s
Loop While (randnum <> 6)
```

▐▐▐➡ As demonstrated, the only change between While and Until is the inverted phrasing of the conditional expression. That is, rather than saying 'Loop Until (randnum = 6)' we simply prefer saying 'Loop While (randnum <> 6)'. Nevertheless, the function remains identical.

Lists and arrays

There are situations where you may change the content of a List during runtime using an InLine script. In those situations, the data type **Array** may be very useful. Let's first consider how to change the content of a List during runtime.

Changing the content of a list

The List below shows some English emotional words typed in during design time.

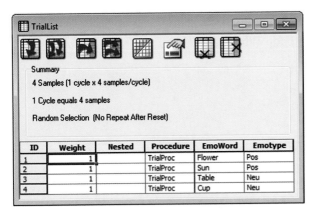

However, the researcher now decides that (s)he wants to be able to change the emotional words of the List into Dutch words during runtime using an InLine script. The following lines of code demonstrate how you can overwrite the English EmoWords (entered during design time) in rows 1 to 4, replacing them with Dutch words during runtime. Of course, this code should run in an InLine object before the List itself is executed.

```
TrialList.SetAttrib 1, "EmoWord", "Bloem"
TrialList.SetAttrib 2, "EmoWord", "Zon"
TrialList.SetAttrib 3, "EmoWord", "Tafel"
TrialList.SetAttrib 4, "EmoWord", "Kom"
```

The syntax of the **<ListName>.SetAttrib** command is:

```
<ListName>.SetAttrib <LevelNumber>, "<Name of the attribute to be saved in>",
<string value to save>
```

➡ Note the important difference with the **c.SetAttrib** command we learned to use earlier. The **<ListName>.SetAttrib** command needs a level number to be specified (i.e. the row number / ID in the List), whereas the c.SetAttrib command only saves the attribute in the current context not in the List itself. The <ListName>.SetAttrib command doesn't depend on the experimental context, but really changes the values in the List itself.

Furthermore, to get some attribute information from a particular row (level) in the List, we can call the **<ListName>.GetAttrib()** function using this syntax.

```
<StringName> = <ListName>.GetAttrib(<LevelNumber>, "<Name of the attribute to
be retrieved>")
```

Given the repetitive structure, you may already have considered that it is helpful to use a For-Next loop in this case. The following code provides an important starting point:

```
Dim Counter As Integer
For Counter = 1 To 4
    TrialList.SetAttrib Counter, "EmoWord", <TODO>
Next
```

So, we simply replace the numbers 1 to 4 using the variable Counter that is integrated in the For-Next loop. However, we still need to fill in the words 'Bloem', 'Zon', 'Tafel', and 'Kom' in the <TODO> part. Of course, one thing we could do is save these String values in four separate variables first, and then use some conditional expressions to maintain the loop structure:

```
Dim S1 As String
Dim S2 As String
Dim S3 As String
Dim S4 As String
S1 = "Bloem"
S2 = "Zon"
S3 = "Tafel"
S4 = "Kom"
'start of the loop
Dim Counter As Integer
For Counter = 1 To 4
    If Counter = 1 Then
        TrialList.SetAttrib Counter, "EmoWord", S1
    End If
    If Counter = 2 Then
        TrialList.SetAttrib Counter, "EmoWord", S2
    End If

    If Counter = 3 Then
        TrialList.SetAttrib Counter, "EmoWord", S3
    End If
    If Counter = 4 Then
        TrialList.SetAttrib Counter, "EmoWord", S4
    End If
Next
```

However, this code is awkward, long and very inflexible. What we actually need in this situation is a new variable type called an 'Array'.

Declaring and using Arrays

An **Array** is a data structure consisting of elements that can be accessed by means of an index number. Think of it as being a column in an Excel file. A very simple example would be the following Array of Strings. You would be able to reach an element of this Array by typing the name of the Array and, in round brackets, the *number of the element.*

ElementNr	Content
1	"Bloem"
2	"Zon"
3	"Tafel"
4	"Kom"

Suppose this Array is called 'WordArray', then you can retrieve the String 'Tafel' by referring to WordArray(3). For instance,

```
Debug.Print WordArray(3)
```

will print "Tafel" in the output screen.

As is the case for all variables in E-Basic, you first have to *declare* an Array before you can assign values to it. During declaration you have to specify what type of an Array you would like to create (Integer, String, etc.) and the number of elements. The kind of Array we declare in this way is called a static Array as you provide a predetermined number of elements (you can also declare *dynamic* Arrays with variable length, but that is outside the scope of this chapter). Okay, let's declare the WordArray with four elements:

```
Dim WordArray(1 to 4) As String
```

So, we have declared an Array named 'WordArray' consisting of four elements (numbers 1 to 4) of the variable type String. That is, the Array is one-based. This is not as self-evident as it may seem: most programming languages, including E-Basic, use zero-based Arrays by default, i.e. the first element is the 0th index.

This is the syntax for Array declaration:

```
Dim <ArrayName>(<number_of_elements>) As <TypeOfVariable>
```

which declares an Array of N elements that run from index o to index <number_of_elements>. Many people find the type of syntax above much more consistent with common speaking habits (imagine the confusion: 'You are first born? So, who is your older sibling?'), and thus prefer to define Arrays as:

```
Dim <ArrayName>(<first index> To <last index>) As <TypeOfVariable>
```

How can we fill these elements with valuable data? Well, we do roughly the same as for a normal variable. However, now we need to refer to the Array name and use an element number:

```
WordArray(1) = "Bloem"
```

Let's now try to declare the abovementioned Array in E-Basic. We fill it with the elements described in the table. So this is the code we need:

```
Dim WordArray(1 To 4) As String
WordArray(1) = "Bloem"
WordArray(2) = "Zon"
WordArray(3) = "Tafel"
WordArray(4) = "Kom"
```

As a next step, we may combine the assignment of elements in the Array with a loop. For example, we can ask the user to provide the content of the Strings rather than letting them be hard-coded. See the example below:

```
Dim WordArray(1 To 4) As String
Dim Counter As Integer
Dim s As String
For Counter = 1 To 4
    s = InputBox("Please enter word no. " & CStr(Counter),"EmoWords Entry")
    WordArray(Counter) = s
Next
```

So, here an InputBox is presented four times. The user's input is temporarily stored in s and then saved in the WordArray, while the Counter variable indicates the number of the element in this Array in which the String will be stored.

Combining Arrays and Lists

Let's now return to our original example, where we planned to change the content of a List during runtime.

The problem we encountered was to efficiently refer to the Dutch emotional words in the <TODO> part of the script below.

```
Dim Counter As Integer
For Counter = 1 To 4
    TrialList.SetAttrib Counter, "EmoWord", <TODO>
Next
```

Given that we now know how to use Arrays, we can solve the problem easily: we simply refer to the Dutch words, using a WordArray, with the variable Counter referring to the *element number* in the Array. In other words, we refer to WordArray(Counter) in the <TODO> part, like in the code below:

```
Dim WordArray(1 To 4) As String
WordArray(1) = "Bloem"
WordArray(2) = "Zon"
WordArray(3) = "Tafel"
WordArray(4) = "Kom"
'Save the data from the array into the list
Dim Counter As Integer
For Counter = 1 To 4
    TrialList.SetAttrib Counter, "EmoWord", WordArray(Counter)
Next
```

This example demonstrates how straightforward it is to combine the For-Next loop with Arrays and Lists.

We can now also let the user decide what words should be saved in the List. Combining the code from the previous section, this should work:

```
Dim WordArray(4) As String
Dim Counter As Integer
Dim s As String
'Fill the array using user input
For Counter = 1 To 4
    s = InputBox("Please enter word no. " & CStr(Counter),"EmoWords Entry")
    WordArray(Counter) = s
Next
'Save the data from the array into the list
For Counter = 1 To 4
    TrialList.SetAttrib Counter, "EmoWord", WordArray(Counter)
Next
```

As you may have noticed already, this code is very flexible. For example, if you would like to change the number of words to be entered because you extended the number of rows in the List, you only need to replace the three '4's in your script with the new number of words to be queried.

Arrays of a user-defined data type

The elements of Arrays are not necessarily confined to standard variable types like Integers, Booleans, Strings and Singles; they can also include a user-defined data type.

Assume you would like to create a variable that stores **address book**-related information such as the name of the person, his/her address, and his/her age. See the example below:

ElementNr	Name	Address	Age
1	"Henk"	"Pelikaanhof 10z"	20
2	"Michiel"	"Suvilahti 1"	32
3	"Jun"	"Rapenburg 440"	30
4	"Rinus"	"Inlinelaan 25u"	23
5	"Saskia"	"Haagweg 50s"	24

What you need in this case is an Array consisting of five elements. Notably, each element should include a Name, an Address and an Age **field**.

What we can do in this case is use the **Type statement** to declare a **user-defined** PersonInfo data type. Important note: Type declaration must always be done *in the User Script*!

```
Type PersonInfo                    'declare new datatype called PersonInfo
    Name As String
    Address As String
    Age As Integer
End Type
```

So this self-defined datatype called 'PersonInfo' consists of three fields of different data types.

Once the datatype has been declared, the Dim command can now be used to declare a new instance of this type. In our case, we declare an Array called 'AddressBook':

```
Dim AddressBook(1 to 5) As PersonInfo
```

Note that the *data type* in this declaration mentions the new user-defined type *PersonInfo* we just declared.

Now we can simply refer to a particular field in the Array using the **dot operator**. For example, to store information in the AddressBook Array for element number 3, we do this:

```
AddressBook(3).Name = "Jun"
AddressBook(3).Address = "The Lake 1"
AddressBook(3).Age = 30
```

Or, to retrieve the age of the person in element number 5, we can use this code:

```
Dim AgeOfThisPerson As Integer
AgeOfThisPerson = AddressBook(5).Age
```

As will be shown in the tutorial, user-defined data types are extremely useful in E-Basic when you would like to modify two or more attributes in a List using Arrays.

Tutorial IX: Quasi-random trial selection

Lists in E-Prime® work well as long as you need sequential or completely random selection, but what happens if you need random selection with particular constraints? This not-quite-random type of selection is in common parlance (amongst psychologists!) sometimes incorrectly referred to as 'pseudo-random'. Given that E-Prime's random-number generator, (much like most other software's), still relies on deterministic processes to produce random numbers, the generator can only approach statistical randomness, but never *be* truly random. However, E-Prime® also doesn't have a simple option for random-with constraints, or *quasi-random* selection or something like that. Although E-Prime 2 does have a feature of 'No Repeat After Reset', usually you will have to program your custom constraints yourself in InLine scripts using For-Next loops and Arrays.

In this tutorial, we will illustrate one way to create a quasi-random sequence of trials, with the constraint being that no two consecutive trials present the same stimulus. This tutorial basically allows you to build the 'No Repeats on Consecutive Trials (Individual Trial)' sample from the E-Prime® Support page programmed by Matt Lenhart, PST (www.pstnet.com/support/login.asp). Understanding all the basic steps will allow you to use an adapted version of the program for your own experiments.

Step 1: Build the basic design

Let's first build the basic design without the sequential constraint. First program the following setup. Use the information presented in the screenshots:

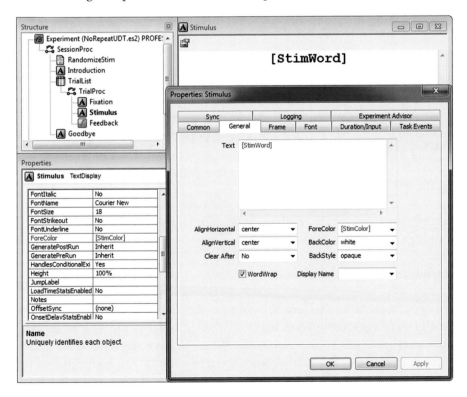

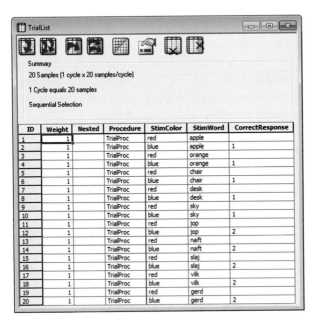

Use the StimColor attribute to set the ForeColor of the Stimulus Object and set the duration of the Fixation and FeedbackDisplays to 750 ms. Add the following information in the introduction screen:

> Welcome. This example experiment demonstrates a method used to prevent trials with an identical condition from repeating on consecutive trials.
>
> You will be presented with a text string. When the text string is blue, your goal is to determine if the text string is a word (1 key) or a non-word (2 key). When the text string is red, don't respond.
>
> Press the spacebar to begin.

Run the experiment and check whether the sequential selection and the trial presentation and feedback work correctly.

Step 2: Randomize the order of the stimuli

Okay, now let's implement random selection in the TrialList with the constraint that a stimulus word is never presented two times in succession: The same word is never presented on two consecutive trials. What we basically need is an InLine object containing E-Basic code that defines the trial order at the beginning of the experiment. The E-Basic code should randomly shuffle the rows in the TrialList, until a random sequence is found that meets the constraint criterion (i.e. no Stim-Word repetition on two consecutive trials).

Please add an InLine object at the start of the SessionProc and name it 'RandomiseStim'.

Let's think before we code. What steps have actually to be programmed in the InLine? Below you will find a proposal:

1   Declare type, Array and other variables we need.

2   Save the information from the List to the Array.

3   Shuffle the content of the Array until the constraint criterion is met.

4   Save the information from the Array back to the List.

5   Run the List.

Please note that we use an Array variable here to store information (from the List), do some manipulations on the Array (shuffling the content), and finally write its content back to the List.

Step 2.1: Declare variables

What kind of variables do we need? The most important variable is the Array, which should temporarily store the information from the List. Given that we need to store three attributes, let's first create a user-defined data type referring to these attribute names in the User Script. To prevent confusion, we keep the attribute and field name identical, although this really is not compulsory:

```
'Create a User-Defined data type to hold the various trial info
Type StimulusData
    StimWord As String
    StimColour As String
    CorrectResponse As String
    'More properties can be added here if necessary.
End Type
```

Okay, that is done. We will now refer to this data type when declaring our *arrStim* variable, the Array that should temporarily store all the information entered into the TrialList during design time. Thus, arrStim is used to keep all of the information about each trial (e.g. stimulus text, stimulus colour, etc.) organised under a single variable. Given that the TrialList consists of 20 rows (trials), we also need 20 elements in our Array:

```
'Declare an array of 20 slots that will hold the User-Defined
'Type created on the User tab of the Script window.
Dim arrStim(20) As StimulusData
```

Please add this declaration to your Inline object *RandomizeStim*,

Step 2.2: Store list content into array

The next step is to retrieve the data from the TrialList and store the attributes into the appropriate field of the Array. We will use the **<ListName>.GetAttrib()** function to retrieve information from the List.

This is how we may implement this:

```
arrStim(1).StimWord = TrialList.GetAttrib(1, "StimWord")
arrStim(1).StimColour = TrialList.GetAttrib(1, "StimColour")
arrStim(1).CorrectResponse = TrialList.GetAttrib(1, "CorrectResponse")

arrStim(2).StimWord = TrialList.GetAttrib(2, "StimWord")
arrStim(2).StimColour = TrialList.GetAttrib(2, "StimColour")
arrStim(2).CorrectResponse = TrialList.GetAttrib(2, "CorrectResponse")
'... et cetera
```

However, given that this would imply copy-pasting and producing (20 repetitions x 3 =) 60 lines of code, it is much better to use a For-Next loop here. The *nCount* variable here runs from number 1 to 20, i.e. each individual trial is loaded into the *arrStim* Array:

```
'Load the stimuli into the array from the TrialList. If your experiment uses
'more properties than the sample, you will also need to load those properties
'as well.
Dim nCount As Integer
For nCount = 1 To 20
    arrStim(nCount).StimWord = TrialList.GetAttrib(nCount, "StimWord")
    arrStim(nCount).StimColour = TrialList.GetAttrib(nCount, "StimColour")
    arrStim(nCount).CorrectResponse = TrialList.GetAttrib(nCount,_
    "CorrectResponse")
Next
```

Please add this code to your Inline object.

Step 2.3: Shuffle the content

We now reach the most important and most difficult step. We will skip this part for now and continue implementing the other parts.

Just add a comment into your InLine script to remind you that the code for this step should be implemented later:

```
'STEP 2-3: Shuffle the content
'This is the difficult part, TODO later!
```

Step 2.4: Store array content into list

Let's assume that the code in the previous step will eventually be successful in creating an Array with its content shuffled across elements. What we then need to do is write the new values of the Array back to the TrialList. This code is very similar to the code in Step 2.2. However, the order is reversed: we now use <List-Name>.SetAttrib to store the values from the Array into the TrialList:

```
'Apply the randomised trial order to the TrialList.
For nCount = 1 To 20
    TrialList.SetAttrib nCount, "StimWord", arrStim(nCount).StimWord
    TrialList.SetAttrib nCount, "StimColour", arrStim(nCount).StimColour
    TrialList.SetAttrib nCount, "CorrectResponse", _
    arrStim(nCount).CorrectResponse
Next nCount
```

Please add this code to your Inline object.

Step 2.5: Run the list

This is a very simple step. Given that the TrialList was added into the Sessionproc during Step 1, it will be run automatically after the InLine object and the instruction screen are run. There is one caveat: given that the preceding steps in the InLine code changed the content of the TrialList, it may need a reset command before it will show the new sequence. So, close your InLine script with this line of code:

```
TrialList.Reset
```

Now we are sure the new content of the Array will be applied correctly to the TrialList when it is going to run. We are ready to start our experiment. Try it out to see if it runs correctly!

If everything is coded correctly, you should observe the same trial sequence as before the InLine script was added. This is simply because we still need to implement the most important step: shuffling the content of the arrStim! Let's face the challenge!

Step 3: Shuffling the order of trials

So, let's return to the part in your InLine script showing this comment:

```
'STEP 2-3: Shuffle the content
'This is the difficult part, TODO later!
```

We need to add some code that randomly shuffles the elements in the arrStim *until* the new Array content meets the sequence constraints. That situation sounds familiar, right? What we need is a loop that runs one or more times until a good sequence is found. We are going to use a 'flag' variable called 'boolCriterion', which remembers whether the sequence is valid.

The flowchart below shows the functionality needed:

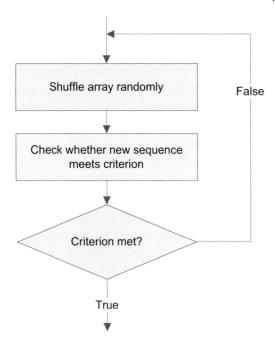

We use the **RandomizeArray** command to shuffle the content of the elements of the Array. This is how the loop translates into E-Basic code:

```
'This variable will be True when the criterion has been met.
Dim boolCriterion As Boolean
'Randomise the array and check for repeated types in consecutive slots. If
'any repeated types are found, set the criterion to False.
Do
    boolCriterion = True
    'Randomise the array (only indices 1-20).
    RandomiseArray arrStim, 1, 20
    'TODO Check to make sure no two trials of the same type in a row.
    'TODO set boolCriterion to False if sequence is not ok
Loop Until boolCriterion = True
```

Replace the STEP 2-3 comment with this code.

Step 4: Check whether sequence meets criterion

We are almost done. The only thing we still need to do is to set the boolCriterion variable to *False* if the sequence in the Array doesn't match the criterion.

Recall that our task was to create a random sequence where a stimulus word is never presented two times in succession.

Again, let's think before we code. What we actually would like to check is whether there is any *Trial n* where StimWord in *Trial n* is the same as the StimWord in *Trial n+1*. Here *n* should run from trial 1 until trial 19 (not 20 because that trial doesn't have a successor).

So, what we need is an extra For-Next loop that runs sequentially through the Array starting with row 1 and running until row 19 to check whether the criterion holds for all rows.

The table below shows a possible result after the Array was randomly shuffled for the first time:

ElementNr	Current Element	Next element
1	jop	naft
2	naft	apple
3	apple	sky
4	sky	slaj
5	slaj	jop
6	jop	chair

ElementNr	Current Element	Next element
7	chair	vilk
8	vilk	slaj
9	slaj	desk
10	desk	apple
11	apple	sky
12	sky	gerd
13	gerd	desk
14	desk	vilk
15	vilk	naft
16	naft	chair
17	chair	orange
18	orange	orange
19	orange	gerd
20	gerd	

As the program loops through elements 1 to 19, it should notice at trial 18 that the subsequent trial has an identical StimWord. Consequently, it should set boolCriterion to *False*. Because of the conditional expression defined in the Loop Until part (see previous step) this will trigger a new loop through the randomisation and check procedure.

Note that the script described in the previous step already gave boolCriterion the *standard value of True before the loop was entered*. So the computer simply starts with the assumption that the sequence is valid. Then, each single cycle through the loop can make the computer change its mind.

This is the code we need in order to set boolCriterion to *False*; that is, whenever it finds the StimWord is identical for two subsequent elements.

```
'Check to make sure no two trials with the same word in a row.
For nCount = 1 To (20-1)
    If arrStim(nCount).StimWord = arrStim(nCount + 1).StimWord Then
        boolCriterion = False
    End If
Next
```

Please add these lines of code to the correct position in the script. Remove the TODO comments.

➤ While looping through the nineteen elements, it might be indicated more than once that the sequence is not valid. All these calls are taken seriously. Although for some elements the subsequent element might meet the criterion, this simply is not relevant here (which is the reason why we never set boolCriterian back to *True* in the loop). If there is at least one single instance of violation, this will be remembered throughout the loop (boolCriterian = *False*) and this will trigger a new loop through the randomisation and check procedure.

We have finished! Check whether the algorithm works correctly by running the experiment.

Exercises

• Add an additional criterion to the quasi-random sequence created in the tutorial: create a random sequence where a stimulus word is never presented two times in succession (like in the tutorial) *and* where the same stimulus colour never appears three times in succession.

• When adapting the tutorial to your own experiment, note that some Lists of stimuli may not be easily randomised, especially if you have a very small number of choices. Occasionally it may not be possible to meet the constraints on the randomisation. If the script in the experiment continues to try to randomise to meet those constraints and is unable to do so, the experiment may appear to freeze. To prevent the possibility of infinite loops, modify the loop: allowing it to exit after 1000 number of retries. In case this happens, show a message box to the user indicating that the randomisation Procedure was not successful and use the End statement to stop the experiment. Test the program by using a criterion that is impossible to meet (e.g. the colour should always be repeated on two consecutive trials).

Advanced exercises

• Use the For-Next loop described in this chapter to further improve the working memory task you adapted during the exercises in Chapter V (using the colour feedback). Add different working memory load conditions of 4, 6, 8 and 10 characters, which are presented in *four* random ordered blocks consisting of *ten* trials each.

Chapter VII

Interactions between Slide objects and the Mouse

In this chapter, you will learn

About: • Common properties and methods of the Slide object
        • Accessing the mouse in E-Prime®
        • Programming user interactions in E-Prime®

How to: • Program a simple questionnaire
         • Program a mouse tracking task

Dear reader, let's assume you have got all the way through six chapters full of useful information and are now well able to code your very own reaction time experiment. However, in order to dazzle your peers even more with something more beautiful, interactive and indeed, 'flashy', in this chapter we will start to go beyond the very basic 80s type of cognitive experiment and will include fancy new hardware, like the mouse, and aspects of more qualitative research; that is, the questionnaire.

It is important to remember that E-Prime's greater strength lies in critical timing and interaction with apparatuses that require such timing, like EEG or eye-tracking. So, when you find yourself mainly involved in questions such as 'how 'betrayed', on a level of 1 to 5, does our participant feel?', or want to test efficacy of immersive user-interfaces combining drag-and-drop behaviour for mobile communication technology, E-Prime® may not be the platform of choice. For indeed, the simple Windows event of 'the user clicked on button A' is not defined within a second of work; whereas web-questionnaires are incredibly easy to make using simple websites.

However, we often find it useful (or sometimes just fun) to add aspects of interactivity, say, one or two clickable objects, to our well-timed experiments. Also, it can be useful to have all the data – including questionnaires – regarding one participant in one place. It certainly beats the alternative: the ultimate boredom of transposing the pen-and-paper data into SPSS!

Therefore, in this chapter we will show you how to engage Slide objects to a deeper extent, how to create a simple questionnaire using E-Prime® and, finally, how to do 'fun stuff' with the mouse.

The Slide object

Slide objects are extremely useful because they allow you to combine text, images, sounds and movies in one and the same object. In this chapter we will learn to access the Slide, including its SlideStates and sub-objects using InLine codes.

Remember that E-Basic is an object-oriented programming language, and that you can refer to properties and methods of particular objects using the *dot operator*. Likewise, you can also read or change properties, and call methods of Slides and their sub-objects.

Let's first consider the hierarchical structure of a Slide object. The figure below shows a Slide object ('Slide1') with a particular SlideState ('Default') including two sub-objects: a SlideText ('Text1') and a SlideImage ('Image1').

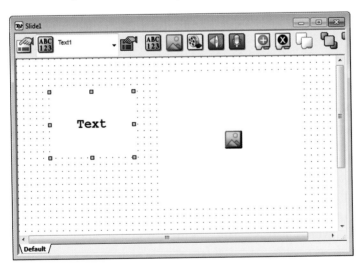

When a Slide is created, E-Basic automatically declares a hierarchical object consisting of the following elements:

Slide1 As Slide
  Default As SlideState
    Text1 As SlideText
    Image1 As SlideImage

For each level in the hierarchy we can access particular properties and methods in E-Basic. A full Listing of all properties and methods can be found in the E-Basic help file. In the subsequent sections we will describe some common examples for each level in the hierarchy.

Slide object: Properties and methods

To read or change the ActiveState we simply refer to the property:

```
Slide1.ActiveState
```

Similarly, if we want to call up the Procedure that manually draws the Slide1 object on the screen (application to be discussed shortly), we may use the method.

```
Slide1.Draw
```

SlideState object: Properties and methods

At the SlideState level, we can control several settings defining its display frame, colours and border. For example, to change the BackColor in the state "Default" of the Slide object "Slide1" to *red* (using a CColour conversion function), we can use this code:

```
Slide1.States("Default").BackColour = CColour("Red")
```

Note that we refer here to the subordinate SlideState "Default" via the property States of the Slide object. The code demonstrates how to access the nested object in E-Basic.

The method HitTest is typically used in conjunction with mouse input. If you provide some coordinates in pixels, the HitTest method will return the String name of a sub-object of Slide (e.g. a SlideImage or a SlideText) at the specified coordinates. If no SlideImage or SlideText object exists at the specified coordinates, an empty String "" is returned.

```
Debug.print Slide1.States("Default").HitTest(400, 300)
```

So, if we run this line of code in an experiment with a screen resolution of 800 x 600 pixels and an object called Image2 is presented in Slide1 at the centre of the screen, the String "Image2" would appear in the debugging window.

Sub-objects within a SlideState: Properties and methods

In order to access SlideText and SlideImage sub-objects in a particular SlideState, you can refer to them via the objects property of a given SlideState. However, before you can read or change properties of a sub-object, you need a temporary variable which references the sub-object.

```
Dim theSlideText As SlideText
Set theSlideText = CSlideText(Slide1.States("Default").Objects("Text1"))
```

So, in the first line we declare our temporary variable of the type SlideText. Then, in the second line we use **Set** to make a reference to the particular SlideText and use the CSlideText casting function to interpret the Text1 object as having the data type SlideText (if you want to learn more about casting functions, check the E-Basic help file).

Now, we can change, for instance, the BorderWidth of the just referenced Slide-Text (so in this example SlideText "Text1" in the "Default" state of "Slide1") by adding the following line of code:

```
theSlideText.BorderWidth = 3
```

Similarly, you can also cast a SlideImage, by simply adapting the variable declaration and casting part. Here is an example:

```
Dim theSlideImage As SlideImage
Set theSlideImage = CSlideImage(Slide1.States("Default").Objects("Image1"))
```

Then, you may change, for instance, the filename associated with the image (so in this example SlideImage "Image1" in the "Default" state of "Slide1"), using this line of code:

```
theSlideImage.FileName = "newfile.bmp"
```

As you can imagine, a similar Procedure is available for other sub-objects such as Sounds and Movies. For more information about all properties and methods available for Slide sub-objects, please refer to the E-Basic Help file.

Accessing the mouse in E-Prime®

The **mouse** is an interesting device as soon as you would like to add complicated hand movements or include questionnaires in E-Prime®. In the Properties of your Experiment, the mouse is activated by default, but its cursor is usually not shown. To change this, simply set the **Show Cursor** property to *Yes*, as indicated in the figure below:

However, showing a mouse cursor is often annoying when you run an experiment that depends on manual responses. So might it not be better to toggle the cursor on and off, depending on the particular time point in the experiment? Well, that is a good idea and pretty easy to do.

To show the mouse cursor on the screen, use the **ShowCursor** method, like this:

```
Mouse.ShowCursor True
```

And to hide it, use this code:

```
Mouse.ShowCursor False
```

Another useful property you may often need is to read the mouse coordinates in pixels. Simply use its CursorX and CursorY properties, as is shown in the example below:

```
Debug.Print Mouse.CursorX
Debug.Print Mouse.CursorY
```

Programming user interactions

There are a number of situations where we may feel the need to combine mouse input and Slide objects. These basically boil down to two major possibilities:

1. You would like to show feedback immediately after a button or mouse click. Unless an exit criterion is met, feedback should be continuously presented on the screen.

2. You would like to have *instant* (not only following a button or mouse click) and continuous online control over your Slide.

The sections below describe both basic setups and their principles. Use them as templates; they can easily be adapted to suit your own needs.

Continuous feedback after mouse clicks

Refreshing a Slide object after a mouse click is something you may want to do when programming questionnaires, visual analogue scales, or other types of mouse pointing-and-clicking tasks.

Imagine you would like to show some visual feedback immediately after a user makes a left-button mouse click in a Slide object, and this Procedure should be repeated again and again until the user clicks with the other (right) mouse button. As feedback, the SlideText position should move to the position of the mouse cursor after each mouse click.

To implement this, we need three objects: a Label, a Slide object, and an InLine object. In addition, add a SlideText sub-object to the default Slide state. See the examples below.

Make sure to set the Slide Duration to *Infinite* and Terminate after the user made a mouse click. Also set ShowCursor to Yes in the experimental properties.

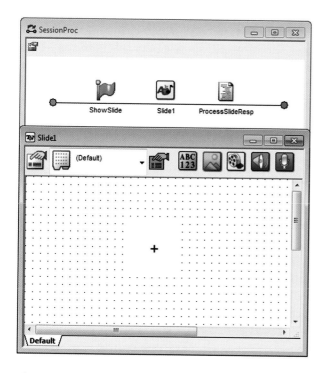

This is the code we need in the ProcessSlideResp Inline object:

```
If Slide1.InputMasks.Responses.Count > 0 Then
    'Get the mouse response
    Dim theMouseResponseData As MouseResponseData
    Set theMouseResponseData = _
      CMouseResponseData(Slide1.InputMasks.Responses(1))
    If theMouseResponseData.RESP = "1" Then
        Dim theSlideText As SlideText
        Set theSlideText = _
          CSlideText(Slide1.States("Default").Objects("Text1"))
        theSlideText.X = theMouseResponseData.CursorX
        theSlideText.Y = theMouseResponseData.CursorY
    Else
        'Exit criterion, stop the experiment
        End
    End If
End If
GoTo ShowSlide
```

In this case, the Goto command at the bottom of the code creates a loop, which triggers a continuous refreshing of the content of the Slide object each time the user makes a mouse click.

The script introduces a MouseResponseData object, which can be used to read the mouse position and responses. The MouseResponseData refers to the object InputMasks.Responses(1), which does the actual response logging of the Slide object. If you would like to learn more about the InputMask object, please study its complicated details in the E-Basic Help file.

Continous online control

Some situations require you to have online access to a device and instantly refresh the Slide object. For example, if you would like to program an approach / avoidance task where you can pull towards (enlarge) or push away (shrink) images with a joystick, you need to sample mouse or joystick data as fast as possible and instantly refresh the screen according to the new cursor position. Other examples are mouse tracking tasks and implicit learning tasks that read complicated hand movements using the mouse or other devices.

The code below shows the basic programming flow you need when you would like to update a SlideText's position instantly. In this case, the position is matched to the position of the mouse cursor instantly (i.e. whenever the mouse is moved, the display is updated immediately). This Procedure described below runs in a Slide object for 10 seconds.

To have continuous online control, we use the InLine object again. To show the display we use the Slide1 object, which is constantly redrawn by our script. See the example below:

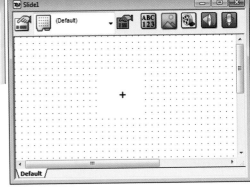

⟶ Make sure you set the Slide Duration to 0! Note that there is still the possibility to log responses: simply set the Time Limit to the value you prefer (i.e. a value >0).

Also set ShowCursor to *Yes* in the experimental properties.

This is the content of the ProcessSlideResp InLine object you need:

```
Dim theSlideText As SlideText
Do While (Clock.Read - Slide1.OnsetTime) < 10000
    Set theSlideText = CSlideText(Slide1.States("Default").Objects("Text1"))
    theSlideText.X = Mouse.CursorX
    theSlideText.Y = Mouse.CursorY
    Slide1.Draw
    Display.WaitForVerticalBlank
    Sleep 10
Loop
```

The Do-While Loop structure here repeats drawing Slide1 again and again, until 10,000 ms (10 seconds) since the Slide1.OnsetTime has passed. However, given that it is useless having faster loops than the screen refresh rate, we decided to add a Display.WaitForVerticalBlank statement and a sleep command to create a loop that is simply as fast as (but not faster than) the refresh rate of the monitor.

⟶ In case you also want to terminate the loop whenever the user makes a button press, simply changing the device's End Action to Terminate will not work. Instead, you have to add an additional criterion to the loop checking whether StimSlide.InputMasks.IsPending() is *True*. As soon as IsPending() gets the value *False*, you know that a response was made or the Time Limit was exceeded.

Tutorial X: A simple questionnaire

Let's program a simple Questionnaire in E-Prime®! The ItemList determines which questions and answers should be presented. The participant is allowed to make multiple selections. Selected items need to be indicated by a black border.

Note that we basically can adapt the 'continuous feedback after mouse clicks' design proposed in this chapter.

Step 1: The basic design

Program the design as depicted in the figures below.

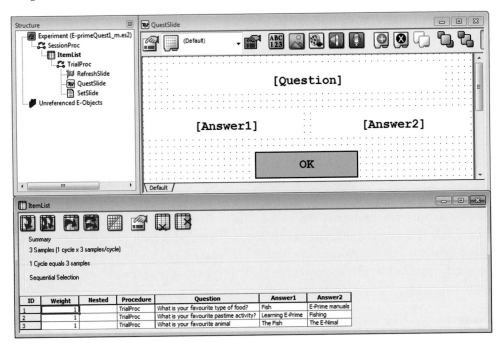

Make sure you set the Slide Duration to *infinite* and terminate after the user makes a mouse click. Also set ShowCursor to *Yes* in the experimental properties.

Name the relevant SlideText objects 'Option1', 'Option2' and 'OKbtn'.

Step 2: Declare variables

Add the following lines of codes to the SetSlide Inline object:

```
Dim Opt1 As SlideText
Dim Opt2 As SlideText
Set Opt1 = CSlideText(QuestSlide.States("Default").Objects("Option1"))
Set Opt2 = CSlideText(QuestSlide.States("Default").Objects("Option2"))
```

In these lines, we create SlideText variables that refer to Option1 and Option2 in the QuestSlide. These variables allow us to later set their property *BorderWidth* to 1 or 0 (indicating whether the particular item is selected).

Step 3: Check the mouse response and do the hit test

The next step is to load the mouse-data response that triggered the termination of the QuestSlide. We first make sure that a response is really made (Responses. Count > 0). In addition, we use the *HitTest* method to know whether the user clicked any object at the specified mouse cursor coordinates. If so, the variable strHit will contain the name of this object.

```
If QuestSlide.InputMasks.Responses.Count > 0 Then
    Dim theMouseResponseData As MouseResponseData
    Set theMouseResponseData = _
    CMouseResponseData(QuestSlide.InputMasks.Responses(1))
    Dim strHit As String
    strHit = QuestSlide.States("Default").HitTest _
    (theMouseResponseData.CursorX, theMouseResponseData.CursorY)
    'process strHit
    'TODO in Step 4
End If
```

Please add these lines of codes to the Inline object.

Step 4: Process the hit test data

Now, consider how to process the hit test data. If the user clicked on Item1, we would like to show some selection/deselection feedback, by adjusting the Border-Width of the respective SlideText object.

To toggle between selection and deselection add these lines of code and remove the comment related to Step 4:

```
If strHit = "Option1" Then
  If Opt1.BorderWidth = 0 Then
    Opt1.BorderWidth = 1
  Else
    Opt1.BorderWidth = 0
  End If
End If
```

Repeat these lines of code for Item2:

```
If strHit = "Option2" Then
   If Opt2.BorderWidth = 0 Then
      Opt2.BorderWidth = 1
   Else
      Opt2.BorderWidth = 0
   End If
End If
```

Step 5: Decide when to refresh the Slide

In the final step we have to consider our exit criterion. When do we want to refresh the Slide object and when do we want to exit the script? Well, the Slide object should always be refreshed unless the hit test reveals that the user clicked the OK-btn object. So, we would like to jump back to the RefreshSlide if strHit <> "OKbtn":

```
If strHit <> "OKbtn" Then
   GoTo RefreshSlide
End If
```

What if the user clicked *OK*? Well, then the program proceeds to the end of the TrialProc and will finish. But, wait a moment! In that case, we may first want to store the selections in the *edat2 file*. To do so, *replace* the If-Then statement mentioned above and add these lines of code to the end of our InLine script:

```
If strHit <> "OKbtn" Then
   GoTo RefreshSlide
Else
   C.SetAttrib "Option1Selected", CStr(Opt1.BorderWidth)
   C.SetAttrib "Option2Selected", CStr(Opt2.BorderWidth)
End If
```

That's it! Test whether your first questionnaire in E-Prime® works appropriately.

Tutorial XI: A mouse tracking task

As a young student you are likely to have efficient motor control over your mouse, but what happens when you become older? Well, it is likely that your motor performance will become impaired. In this tutorial we are going to program a mouse tracking task that may be useful for calculating indices of motor (dis)ability.

This mouse tracking task is an adapted version of the one-dimensional task described by Riviere & Thakor (1996). As shown in the figure on the next page, a stationary vertical line segment (100 pixels) is displayed on the computer screen (1024 x 768 pixels). A small square target oscillates along the right side of the line segment in sinusoidal fashion. The participant tracks the target's motion with a small round mouse cursor, which moves along the left side of the line. The experiment should be programmed such that the X component of the mouse signal is ignored and only the Y component is sampled. In this way, the mouse cursor is constrained to move vertically and is not sensitive to sideways mouse movement. The trial should stop after a mouse click, or in case of omission after 10 seconds.

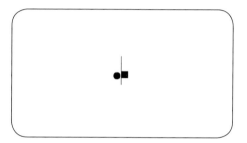

Note that we basically need to adapt the 'continuous online control' design proposed in this chapter.

Step 1: The basic design

Create an E-Prime® experiment including a TrialList and a TrialProc (no attributes defined). Add a Slide object and name it 'TrackingSlide'. Add an InLine object and name it 'ProcStim'.

Set the duration of the TrackingSlide to 0. Add a Mouse Device and set the *Time-Limit* to 10,000 ms.

Add two SlideImages and name them 'Dot' and 'Square', respectively (see the figure above). Create a Dot.bmp and a Square.bmp file in MS Paint (20 x 20 pixels) and load them into the SlideImages.

The line segment can be created using a TextDisplay having a Width of 1 and a Borderwidth of 1.

Make sure the line is presented in the centre of the screen. Align the *X positions* of the Dot and the Square images so that they are presented along the left and right side of the line, respectively.

Step 2: Set the online Slide control

In the ProcStim Inline script, add the following lines of code.

```
Dim CurrTarget As SlideImage
Dim CurrCursor As SlideImage
Set CurrTarget = _
  CSlideImage(TrackingSlide.States("Default").Objects("Square"))
Set CurrCursor = _
  CSlideImage(TrackingSlide.States("Default").Objects("Dot"))
```

These references allow us to later change the *Y position* of the respective SlideImages.

The only part of the code that should be added is shown below:

```
Dim ClockNow As Long
Dim PeriodDur As Single
Dim y As Single
Dim Amplitude As Integer
Amplitude = 20
PeriodDur = 2000 'ms, duration of one period
Do While (TrackingSlide.InputMasks.IsPending())
    ClockNow = Clock.Read
    y = Sin((ClockNow - TrackingSlide.OnsetTime)/PeriodDur*2*pi)
    CurrTarget.Y = (Display.YRes/2) - (Amplitude * y)
    'move cursor
    CurrCursor.Y = Mouse.CursorY
    Display.WaitForVerticalBlank
    TrackingSlide.Draw
    Sleep 10
Loop
```

Let's study these lines of code thoroughly!

The most important structure is the **Do While – Loop** structure, which repeatedly calls the TrackingSlide.Draw method while the mouse response is pending (i.e. no mouse click given and time limit not yet exceeded).

The other important part relates to the lines starting with 'CurrTarget.Y =', and 'CurrCursor.Y ='. Here we change the position of the Square and Dot images in the TrackingSlide object.

Because the target should move in a sinusoidal fashion, we first calculate *y*, which uses the **Sin()** function in combination with the time passed (= ClockNow - TrackingSlide.OnsetTime) and the duration of the period (here 2000 ms) in radials (i.e. * 2 * pi) to produce a value between -1 and +1.

The left panel of the figure below shows a standard sinusoidal function for 1 cycle.

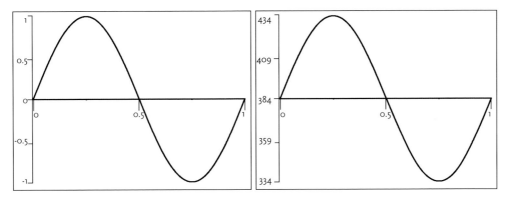

However, given that we would like to calculate the value in pixels measured from the top of the screen, we use the formula (Display.YRes/2) - (Amplitude * y). So, when using a 1024 x 768 resolution we used (768/2) - (50 * y) to produce the sinusoidal movement around the vertical midline on the screen (as shown in the right panel of the figure).

Run the experiment and check whether it works correctly!

▐▶ Note: the variable Duration in the example above has a fixed value throughout the experiment. In such cases you might consider to declare a constant instead, using the **Const** statement. See the E-Basic help file for more information about the **Const** statement.

Exercises

- Add extra trials to the List of the questionnaire in Tutorial X. Add an InLine script to the beginning of the TrialProc to make sure that each question always starts showing all options deselected.

- Disable the possibility of selecting option1 and option2 at the same time, so that the participant is forced to choose one out of two. Draw a flowchart before programming.

- Now adapt the questionnaire in such a way that the participant has to choose one out of eight options. Draw a flowchart before programming.

- The questionnaire you created can be useful as a manipulation check. Add the questionnaire to the end of the Ego depletion experiment (Tutorial V, Chapter III). Ask participants to rate on an 8-points scale how tired, thoughtful, excited, happy, worn out, sad/depressed, angry, and calm they feel at the end of the film viewing task. Make sure the response is stored in the edat file.

- Download the file *E-primeQuestionnaire.es2* from www.e-primer.com. This program shows how you can present one or more sheets of ten questionnaire items on a screen in E-Prime®. Perfect for long questionnaires! The answers given are automatically stored in the edat file (see the attributes *ChosenOption* and *ChosenOptDes*). To ensure a convenient structure in the edat file, the questionnaire was programmed in a roundabout way, needing many Lists, Procedures and InLine (too complicated to explain here). However, the only thing you need to know for now is: Whenever the Procedure *RunOneSheetOf10Items* is executed, it presents the content of 11 consecutive rows (one header + ten items with their options) stored in the *AllQuestionnaires* List.

- Adapt the content of the questionnaire to suit your own needs (e.g. copy-paste a bunch of your favourite personality questionnaires). In order to change the text for the items, just change the content of the *AllQuestionnaires* List (note that row numbers 1-11, 12-22, 23-33, etc. will be presented in separate sheets). ItemIDs fields that are left empty will not be used, neither are option fields that are left empty. Optionally, you can set the PreSelection field, when a particular item number should be preselected in advance.

- Call the Procedure *RunOneSheetOf10Items* at the proper location (in a particular List) in your experiment and repeat this for the number of sheets you would like to present.

- Experiment with changing the content of the *AllQuestionnaires* List and run the questionnaires!

Advanced exercises

- Add additional frequency conditions (1 Hz, 2 Hz and 4 Hz) to the TrialList of the experiment in Tutorial XI and adjust the code so that the value in PeriodDur depends on the given attribute in the List.

- Store the CurrTarget.Y and CurrCursor.Y values in two Arrays. The size should equal the maximum number of cycles through the loop. Each cycle is stored in a separate element of the Array.

- Super advanced level (!): Give feedback about performance at the end of each trial using the Accuracy Index (AI). Riviere & Thakor (1996, p. 9) describe how to calculate this index: (Hint: read 'Arrays' when they refer to 'vectors'; RMS = the root of the mean of the squares of all elements in the Array / vector):

  The position vector of the target on the computer screen was the input to the human sensorimotor system in these tests, referred to as the "target" and represented as t. The motion that the human subject made in response to the target was indicated by the mouse cursor location. This was considered the output, o, of the system. The error vector e was obtained by the equation.

  e = t - o.

  (...)For the 1-D tests, these three are only one-dimensional vectors :

  e = [e_1], t = [t_1], o = [o_1].

  For each test, E and A, the RMS values of the error vector e and the target signal t, respectively, were calculated for each test. The subjects' overall accuracy in tracking was represented by a measure called the "Accuracy Index (AI)". (...)

  In the special case of the 1-D tests, there was no x-component, and the AI could be simplified as

  AI = 1 − E / A

  For all tests, perfectly accurate motion generation resulted in zero error and, therefore, in an AI of unity. Leaving the cursor unmoved in the centre of the screen resulted in a value of zero for AI.

- Check whether your feedback script works correctly!

Chapter VIII

Various Input/Output devices

In this chapter, you will learn

About:
- The PST SRBOX
- The voice-key device
- Sending pulses using the parallel port
- Reading and writing text files

How to:
- Program a voice-key test program
- Program the Knight Rider scanner light

One of the best aspects of E-Prime® is that it is so widely used. As you have noticed from the tutorials, a variety of fields can benefit from the experiments covered here. A simple RT experiment (I) is for the classic chronometrist. The Simon Task (II) remains popular in cognitive psychology and neuroscience. The Implicit Association Task (III) is widely used in social psychology, for example to find out the effect of stereotypes. Sounding a distracting noise while participants are engaged in various types of tasks with varying workloads (IV) can have great importance for the industrial/organisational psychology and the field of Human Computer Interaction. Ego depletion (V) remains a hot topic in social psychology. Working memory tests (VI) are prevalent in clinical and cognitive psychology and neuroscience whilst the Ultimatum game (VII) and Cyberball (VIII) are popular in Economics and social psychology. Questionnaires (IX) are, of course, used in all the various fields across psychology and the Mouse Tracking Test (X) might be useful in clinical and neuropsychology practice.

Thus, E-Prime® is used widely throughout psychological and cognitive science and this comes with a very nice bonus: a number of hardware manufacturers include packages specifically designed for integrating E-Prime® with their equipment. Indeed, PST sell the SRBOX, which comes with five buttons ('multi-touch'), five ('penta-lit') lights, and a microphone input (which harbours the voice key); but, most importantly, it has great temporal accuracy. Other manu-facturers, such as Tobii (an official partner of PST), BrainProducts and EGI, also know E-Prime® well and often offer support and even custom packages for integrating eye-trackers and EEG equipment with your experiment. In this final chapter, you will learn how to interact with various pieces of equipment from within E-Prime®.

The Serial-Response box

The **Serial-Response Box** (SRBOX) comes heavily recommended with an E-Prime® licence. This is, of course, only to be expected since the same people who made E-Prime® also sell this nifty, but rather ugly, little device. Apart from that, they say it comes with timing properties that are far superior to those of other reaction-recording devices – typically keyboards, mice and (with E-Prime 2) joysticks. On the subject of keyboards and mice, in particular, it makes a great deal of difference exactly what kind of response-device you use and how it is connected. Please see www.pstnet.com/ for more information, and find out that PST claims that their SRBOX does quite well in all cases. Whether or not that is the case (and you should test this yourself!), it is cer-tainly true that it is easy to use, considering it comes pre-programmed in E-Prime®, saving us a lot of work and cognitive strain. Moreover, some research-ers use the SRBOX in EEG labs, because it can be connected to buttons that, unlike the standard keyboard, don't interfere with the physiological measure-ments involved.

Our typical SRBOX has five buttons that are horizontally placed on the top of the device, a serial port connection (the one with lots of pins) and a microphone connection. The latter will be discussed in more detail below on the subject of voice-key experiments, but first let's get the thing to work in the simplest way pos-sible.

Adding the SRBOX

We go to *Edit > Experiment > Devices* tab and press the *Add* button. After double-clicking on the *SRBOX* and pressing *OK*, the following screen shows it is now added to the experiment:

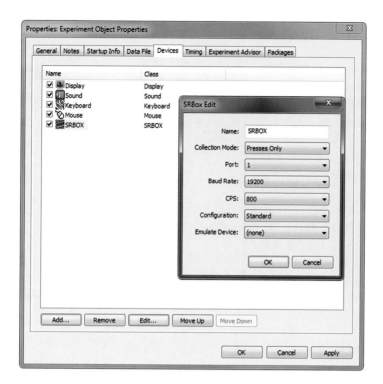

That is to say, this is what you would get if you had also selected *SRBOX* and clicked on *Edit*. The properties are confusing enough, so we will only mention two here:

Collection Mode: Can be set to collect 'releases' and 'presses and releases'. This also applies to most of the other response-capturing devices (such as keyboards and mice) and can be useful if you, for example, have a participant pressing a button before the trial starts, and only want to do something after the button is released.

Port: Refers to the COM port of the computer to which the SRBOX is serially connected. In the good old days, when communication between computers went through serial connection by default, PCs typically had a number of serial ports. Now, it is increasingly rare to find PCs that even have a single one. We will assume the reader has such a port, or uses a USB adapter, and in the meantime, it is usually easier to connect the cable to whatever plug in the computer works and then see if this is the correct port.

If you connect the SRBOX to the power supply, you will notice the lights just above the buttons will light up. Upon running your experiment at this stage, *they should turn off automatically*. If this is not the case, the SRBOX's connection is usually faulty.

Using the SRBOX

Now, clicking on *OK* finalises the first step. On with the question as to how to gather data using the SRBOX, we take a typical stimulus showing object, such as the TextDisplay, go to its properties, select the *Duration / Input* tab and *Add* the SRBOX as a new response-collecting device. By entering '12345' as allowable responses, you allow the SRBOX's buttons to be used for this TextDisplay. Response 1, here, refers to the leftmost button of the SRBox (to your left, if you have placed it with the buttons towards you), 3 to the middle button, and so on.

Voice-key experiments

It turns out the microphone input was, after all, not there for dubious karaoke purposes, but rather to enable you to design voice-key experiments. Using the **voice key** is in many ways not very different from using the SRBOX, except that you attach the microphone to the SRBOX and set the *Allowable Response* to '6'. However, many psychological experiments depend, to a great extent, on the accuracy of the voice key, so we will make an effort here to get you started using it in a *sensible* way.

Stimulus →   Planning →   Utterance

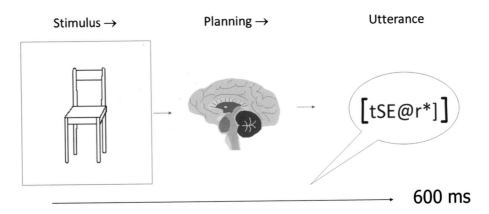

[tSE@r*]]

600 ms

In many psycholinguistic experiments, a voice key (VK) is a valuable tool to measure onset latencies of utterances. If, for instance, you want to measure how much time it takes from seeing a picture of a chair and actually pronouncing the word 'chair' the voice key is the device you will most likely use. It captures how long it takes between presentation of a stimulus and the beginning of an utterance, hopefully precisely the planning process you are interested in.

So, what is a VK anyway? A VK is a device that is situated between a microphone and a (E-Prime® enhanced) computer and measures a participant's vocal reaction time (note: it doesn't record the participant's voice). It monitors the volume level of auditory input coming from an attached microphone. When that volume crosses a certain threshold and stays over that threshold for a certain amount of time it will register this as a participant's reaction time. In the SRBOX a VK is already built in, so there is no need to attach a separate VK. We have already learned that the SRBOX is connected to the PC with a serial (COM) cable. So the next part is: how do we connect a microphone to the SRBOX/VK?

You might think it would be a straightforward answer, just plug the microphone into the microphone input, but that need not necessarily be the case. It depends whether the microphone needs power or not. The SRBOX ships with a separate microphone, which can be attached with no problems as it doesn't require power. However, if one wants to attach a stereo headset microphone, two problems may arise. (1) Some headset microphones may require electrical power to operate, which is normally provided by the computer it is attached to, but the SRBOX doesn't supply that power to the microphone. So, if you have this problem the solution is to 1) buy another headset; or 2) put a small power supply – called an 'electret condenser' (normally used for tie clip microphones) – in between. And (2) the SRBOX seems to accept primarily mono microphones. You can see whether your microphone is stereo or mono by the number of (usually black) 'rings' on the plug of your microphone (1 = mono, 2 = stereo).

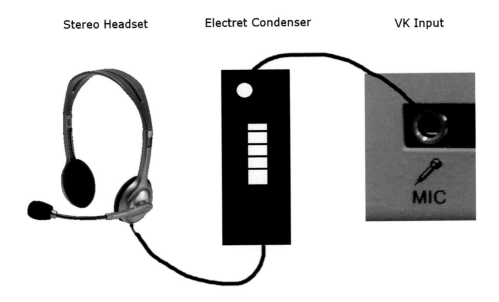

Stereo Headset　　　**Electret Condenser**　　　**VK Input**

Okay, suppose now that everything is working fine technically: the microphone is correctly plugged in and the VK is purring with excitement in awaiting its input. What then? First of all, we need to calibrate and check the VK settings for each participant separately (not everybody's voice is the same). This can be done by presenting a participant with words which he/she is required to read aloud.

Obviously, not all words sound the same. What is especially important for experiments using a VK is to keep in mind that not all onsets of words are equally loud. Words like 'house' and 'prince', for example, have very different onsets. The 'h' in 'house' starts much softer than the 'plosive' 'p' in 'prince', so if you calibrate the VK using only strong onset words but use other words in your real experiment, this would likely lead to non-registered responses.

Also of crucial importance in a VK experiment is the instruction/explanation that is given to the participant. A VK is a 'dumb' machine, meaning that it doesn't know whether auditory input is a voice, or smacking, sighing, rocking the chair about, etc. Many people, without knowing it, exhibit a little 'smack' (caused by opening their mouth or just general drooling) before they speak and/or sometimes breathe loudly before they utter a word or sentence. This can lead to accidental triggering of the VK before the word is actually spoken, which results in an unusable RT. The instruction should therefore clearly indicate that unwanted sounds (i.e. sounds other than spoken words) should be avoided.

In most VK experiments the experiment leader plays a greater role than in a 'normal' experiment. This is because in most cases the experimental leader has to judge whether a trial was valid or invalid. This judgement Procedure is mainly done by inserting a blank TextDisplay with the Duration set to *infinity* to which the experimenter can react with a code (for instance: allowable response is '123'; 1=correct trial, 2=VK error like a 'smack', 3=wrong utterance like saying 'fruit' to 'banana' or something). You may also consider using the **SoundIn** object (new in E-Prime 2), so that you can record the voice and categorise the trials offline.

Sending signals using the parallel port

When using E-Prime® to present stimuli in an experiment that uses psycho-physiological measures (EEG, heart rate, skin conductance, EMG, etc.), you usually want to mark the onset of events from E-Prime® in the stream of physiological data that is acquired. To do so, labs often make use of the good old **parallel port**, also known as the **LPT port**. Before the USB era (in the last century), the parallel port usually connected the computer to external devices such as text printers (LPT stands for Line Print Terminal). However, since the parallel port can be accessed in E-Basic, it is a helpful device to send 8-bit digital signals (a.k.a. markers or pulses) to acquisition devices that store physiological data.

The picture below shows a standard parallel port. Unfortunately, it is not available on all modern computers.

By connecting the eight output pins (indicated by the red colour) to a connector we can link them to electronic devices such as an acquisition device. In the example below, the outputs are connected to LEDs which creates an LPT port testing device:

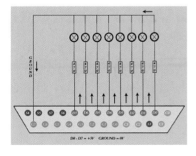

Bits and bytes

Before describing how to send information to the parallel port using E-Basic, let's briefly explain the type of information that can be transferred using the parallel port.

We learned that the LPT port consists of eight output pins. These pins can send an electrical signal of either 0 or 5 Volts, corresponding to a bit value of either being 0 (False) or 1 (True). Because of the eight pins, the LPT port can send eight bits of information which equals 1 Byte (by definition, 1 Byte = 8 bits).

It is important to understand that 8 bits of data allow you to send the decimal numbers 0 until 255. The table below shows the decimal notation of these numbers and how they translate to a binary notation of the 8 bits.

Decimal notation	Binary notation
0	00000000
1	00000001
2	00000010
3	00000011
4	00000100
5	00000101
6	00000110
7	00000111
8	00001000
...	...
250	11111010
251	11111011
252	11111100
253	11111101
254	11111110
255	11111111

You may check how the conversion between decimal and binary notation works, e.g. by using your Windows Calculator (*Scientific view*).

So what happens if you send the decimal signal 250 to the parallel port? Well, this will set the voltage to 5 V for the pins representing the bits that have value 1 (pins D1, D3, D4, D5, D6 and D7), whereas the other pins will get value 0V (pins D0 and D2).

When the device connected at the other side of the cable registers the voltage, it can convert this digital signal back to a decimal number, which then can be used in your analysis software to mark the onset of particular events.

The timeline below shows some activity at pin D0 to D7 (related to bit 0 to bit 7) and the decimal marker that can be derived from it.

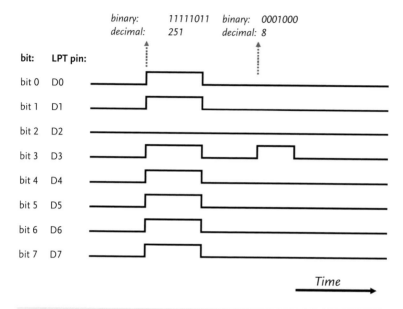

▦➡ It is important to note that, as in this example, the decimal marker is usually only detected at the rising edges of the signal, not at the falling edge (note that this also implies that the duration of the pulse usually is not registered). That is why you should always reset all the lines of the port (i.e. send value 0 to the port) before sending a new pulse. In this example: after code 251 is sent, the port is first set to 0 before it sends the other code 8. Also make sure to use some script to reset the port at the beginning (and end) of your experiment: you can't assume that the LPT port has value 0 by default.

Sending signals to the parallel port

There are two methods to send signals to the parallel port and you may combine both methods in your experiment.

1. Instantly write data to a port
2. Link port data to the onset/offset of an E-Object

The first method is pretty easy. Use the Writeport command in an InLine object to write a value between 0 and 255 to the address of the LPT port.

The example below sends decimal value 0 (all bits reset) to the LPT port address:

```
WritePort 888, 0
```

It is recommended that you always add this line of code at the beginning and end of the experiment, to ensure that the digital port gets a reset before pulses will be sent.

The code below sends a decimal value 10 to the LPT port, using the same address 888:

```
WritePort 888, 10
```

Make sure you set the port back to 0 before sending a new code. For example, to send a 20 ms pulse, you may combine the WritePort command with the **Sleep** command, like in this example.

```
WritePort 888, 10        'send decimal value 10 to LPT port
Sleep 20                 'wait 20 ms
WritePort 888, 0         'reset LPT port to value 0
```

▐▌➡ Note that the LPT port address usually is assigned to decimal number 888 (which is identical to the hexadecimal notation &H378). However, some computers use an alternative address; check the settings of the computer in your lab before running the experiment!

The second method links port data to the *onset* and/or *offset* of particular E-Objects.

Assume you would like to send a data pulse (the decimal value 120) starting at the *onset* of the Stimulus Slide object in the example below.

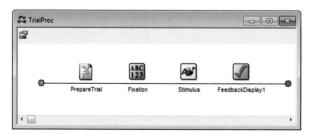

To link the port data to the Stimulus object, you now have to add the following code in the PrepareTrial InLine object:

```
Stimulus.OnsetSignalEnabled = True      'Enable the port settings
Stimulus.OnsetSignalPort = 888          'This is the standard LPT port address
Stimulus.OnsetSignalData = 120          'This is the data pulse / stimulus code
```

The example below shows how you can set different codes depending on a particular experimental condition (let's assume that this is determined by the attribute Condition):

```
Stimulus.OnsetSignalEnabled = True      'Enable the port settings
Stimulus.OnsetSignalPort = 888          'This is the standard LPT port address
If c.GetAttrib("Condition") = "Word" Then
    'Experimental condition: Word
    Stimulus.OnsetSignalData = 120
Else
    'Experimental condition: NonWord
    Stimulus.OnsetSignalData = 100
End If
```

So these lines of code will introduce some rising edges in the parallel port and the values 120 and 100 will be detected by the acquisition device. However, if you have fixed codes for the different conditions, consider adding an attribute e.g. 'LPTcode' to your TrialList and put the value 100 and 120 (or any other values between 0 and 255) at the proper location in the List. Then use the value of this attribute for the OnsetSignalData, like this:

```
Stimulus.OnsetSignalEnabled = True      'Enable the port settings
Stimulus.OnsetSignalPort = 888          'This is the standard LPT port address
Stimulus.OnsetSignalData = CInt(c.GetAttrib("LPTcode"))
```

However, recall that we still need to reset the LPT port before we are allowed to send a new pulse. So we may consider defining a reset signal at the Stimulus' offset (i.e. the time it disappears from the screen):

```
Stimulus.OffsetSignalEnabled = True     'Enable the port settings
Stimulus.OffsetSignalPort = 888         'This is the standard LPT port address
Stimulus.OffsetSignalData = 0           'Reset the port at Stimulus Offset
```

However, there is one important caveat when using the offset method! What would happen if the Stimulus was presented for only 0 ms, either because the duration was set to that value or because a user made an ultrafast response? Well, in that case you created a spike-like pulse lasting less than a millisecond. It is very likely that your acquisition device fails to detect these spikes, simply because the parallel port data can't sample that fast. So, as the designer of the experiment you should make sure that the duration of the object will allow the pulse to stay at least, say, 10 ms (this value should be fine when the sampling rate of the acquisition device is 256 Hz or higher).

Alternatively, you can leave the OffSetSignal disabled (as it is by default) and simply use the reset command in an InLine object placed at the proper location in your experimental time line. In that case, simply use the code we already know:

```
WritePort 888, 0
```

An easier way to link port data to the onset/offset and other events of E-objects has been introduced in E-Prime 2 Professional. Here it is possible to use **Task Events** to write data to the parallel port. As Task Events are beyond the scope of this book, please see the E-Prime® documentation for a more detailed description.

Reading and writing text files

The C.SetAttrib command and the automatic logging in E-Prime® usually do a great job in saving all the data you need. However, in some special cases, it is also possible to manually read and write text files using E-Basic.

Reading a text file

First check whether the file exists using the **FileExists()** function. Then open the text file in the *Read* mode using the **Open** command, such as:

```
If FileExists("P:\\test.txt") Then
    Open "P:\\test.txt" For Input As #1
Else
    MsgBox "P:\\test.txt does not exist"
End If
```

Note that we use double backslashes '\\' in the file path to avoid '\t' being interpreted as a tab character. A recommended alternative is to use a forward slash '/' instead: it may be counter-intuitive to established Microsoft convention, but it is actually more similar to other Operating Systems.

The Open command uses this syntax:

```
Open <Path+FileName.txt> For Input As #<FileNumber>
```

Now we can read the first line in the file using the **Line Input** command, like this:

```
Dim s As String
Line Input #1, s
MsgBox s                        'shows the first line in the textfile
```

With the syntax for Line Input being:

```
Line Input #<FileNumber>, <string to store line into>
```

If you would like to read a complete text file, you need to use the Line Input command in combination with a loop. In that way, you can read the file line by line. Use the **EOF** function to determine whether you reached the End Of File, as in this example:

```
Dim s As String
Do While Not EOF(1)       'do while not end of file #1
    Input #1,s
Loop
MsgBox "The last line was: \n" & s
```

Close the file (indicate the file number) after you are done using the Close command:

```
Close #1
```

Writing to a text file

First check whether the file exists using the **FileExists()** function. Otherwise, the Open command will overwrite the existing file with an empty text file without warning!

```
If Not FileExists("P:\\test.txt") Then
    Open "P:\\test.txt" For Output As #1
Else
    MsgBox "P:\\test.txt already exists!"
End If
```

Here, the Open command uses this syntax:

```
Open <Path+FileName.txt> For Output As #<FileNumber>
```

If you would rather add lines of text to an existing text file, open the file in Append modus using this syntax:

```
Open <Path+FileName.txt> For Append As #<FileNumber>
```

Now, you are ready to print a line of text using the **Print** command:

```
Print #1, "Print this line of text"
```

With the syntax being:

```
Print #<FileNumber>, <stringtoprint>
```

To close the file, use the Close command:

```
Close #1
```

Tutorial XII: Making a Voicekey (VK) test program

To be able to conduct a good VK experiment, you need to establish how to modify the VK and instructions are to be modified for a given participant. We are going to create a simple word naming experiment to test this.

Step 1: The basic Design

Create a test List (16-20 items) with words that have a multitude of onsets (like the well-known Dutch 'aap-noot-mies' table).

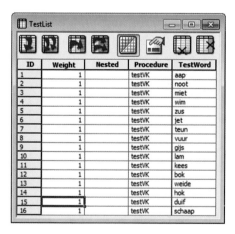

ID	Weight	Nested	Procedure	TestWord
1	1		testVK	aap
2	1		testVK	noot
3	1		testVK	miet
4	1		testVK	wim
5	1		testVK	zus
6	1		testVK	jet
7	1		testVK	teun
8	1		testVK	vuur
9	1		testVK	gijs
10	1		testVK	lam
11	1		testVK	kees
12	1		testVK	bok
13	1		testVK	weide
14	1		testVK	hok
15	1		testVK	duif
16	1		testVK	schaap

Step 2: The trial

The basic trial setup is quite simple: 1) Fixation Cross + (1000ms); 2) TestWord (infinite; allowed SRBOX:6); 3) a feedback screen to see the RT; and 4) a Text-Display containing an asterisk (infinite; allowed keyboard: 123). Set the TestList to present the words randomly (perhaps even twice), also make sure to *add* the SRBOX to the experiment (using experiment object) otherwise it will not show up as a possible response device (also see: 'Adding the SRBOX'). Check whether the *Input Object Name* of the feedback screen is properly set and make sure it only displays an RT and not whether the stimulus was correct or not. For the reading and pronunciation of a written word an average RT spans between 350 and 550ms.

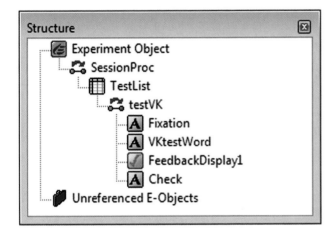

Step 3: Too loud or too soft?

Now run the experiment. Problems occur whenif a participant's voice is too soft (to be registered as a response) or too loud (e.g. if non-utterances trigger the voice key). There are three ways of coping with problems like these. First, you can move the microphone closer to or further away from the mouth of the participant or ask the participant to speak softer or louder. Second, by turning the VK sensitivity knob with a screwdriver, it is possible to adjust its hardware sensitivity. Counter-clockwise turning increases the sensitivity pf the VK threshold and clockwise turning decreases the sensitivity. Last, you can use an InLine to adjust the sensitivity. This can be done by using the following code (where x = a value between 0 and 31; 0 being most and 31 least sensitive).

```
SRBOX.VoicekeyTripLevel = x
```

Note that option two and three work independently, meaning that they can affect one another.

If you notice that a participant, who is asked to speak softer or louder, doesn't follow experimental instructions, and you don't want to cope with a small screw-driver stuck in your SRBOX (why is there no physical knob, oh mighty SRBOX creator?), you might want to build in a statement at the checking part that allows for manipulation of the abovementioned variable.

Step 4: To conclude

The abovementioned VK test experiment might not be the most challenging with respect to programming and design but to perform any valid VK experiment it is essential to control for sound anomalies and to explain to the participant where 'things' can go wrong. Also the checking part for the experimental leader is of utmost importance. Think of the following example: you presented participants the word 'widow' but the word disappeared not on the onset W, but rather on the consonant D from the –W part. This is an invalid trial. As significant psycholin-guistic effects tend to range from 10-50 ms it is essential that the RT of the word (or picture) reflects the onset of the utterance.

Exercises

- Create an experiment that allows you to test activity at the eight pins of the parallel port (you will need a testing device such as the one presented on page 183). Show a stimulus for 1 second on the screen preceded by a fixation point (duration of 500 ms). The stimulus should show the decimal values 1, 2, 4, 8, 16, 32, 64 and 128, respectively and this value should be sent to the LPT port at Stimulus onset. Don't forget to reset the port before sending a new pulse! Test whether your program correctly sends the signals to the LPT port using a parallel port testing device.

Advanced Exercises

- For our final exercise you will recreate the incredible scanner beam emitted by KITT from the Knight Rider television series. This scanner beam is actu-ally a light similar to the previous exercise but now it should start at the left and, when reaching the right, it should then go back to the left. The easiest example is the one shown in the figure on the next page, but if you really want to stretch your skills you may also start out with two lights and then move two lights to the right (and end with two lights on the right and then move back). You may choose to use onset and/or offset of objects or write the whole exercise entirely in one InLine (using writeport).

One light moving

Two lights moving

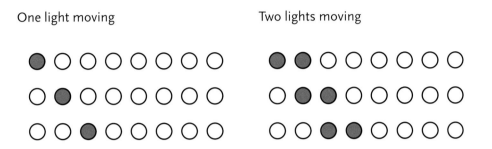

- Note: make sure the whole scanner beam repeats at least five times from left to right to allow KITT enough time to scan the surroundings for enemies.

Reference List

Baumeister, R.F., Bratslavsky, E., Muraven, M. & Tice, D.M. (1998). Ego depletion: Is the active self a limited resource? *Journal of Personality and Social Psychology, 74,* 1252.

Blais, C. (2008). Random without replacement is not random: caveat emptor. *Behavior Research Methods, 40,* 961-968.

Duncan, J. & Humphreys, G.W. (1989). Visual search and stimulus similarity. *Psychological Review, 96,* 433.

Greenwald, A.G., McGhee, D.E. & Schwartz, J.L. (1998). Measuring individual differences in implicit cognition: The implicit association test. *Journal of Personality and Social Psychology, 74,* 1464.

Güth, W., Schmittberger, R. & Schwarze, B. (1982). An experimental analysis of ultimatum bargaining. *Journal of Economic Behavior & Organization, 3,* 367-388.

Luck, S.J. & Vogel, E.K. (1997). The capacity of visual working memory for features and conjunctions. *Nature, 390,* 279-280.

Riviere, C.N. & Thakor, N.V. (1996). Effects of age and disability on tracking tasks with a computer mouse: accuracy and linearity. *Journal of Rehabilitation Research and Development, 33,* 6-15.

Schneider, W., Eschman, A., & Zuccolotto, A. (2002). E-Prime User's Guide. *Psychology Software Tools*: Pittsburgh, PA.

Simon, J.R. & Rudell, A.P. (1967). Auditory SR compatibility: The effect of an irrelevant cue on information processing. *Journal of Applied Psychology, 51,* 300.

Sternberg, S. (1969). Memory-scanning: Mental processes revealed by reaction-time experiments. *American Scientist*, 421-457.

Stroop, J.R. (1935). Studies of interference in serial verbal reactions. *Journal of Experimental Psychology, 18*, 643.

Williams, K.D. & Jarvis, B. (2006). Cyberball: A program for use in research on interpersonal ostracism and acceptance. *Behavior Research Methods, 38*, 174-180.

Appendix: Overview of available E-Objects

Here we provide an overview of all E-Objects, listing their main function and the chapter in which the object is introduced. For a complete overview of all properties of each E-Object, we refer you to the E-Prime 2.0 documentation, which can be downloaded from the E-Prime® support page.

Icon	Name	Description	Chapter
	Procedure	Used to determine the order of events in an experiment.	I
	List	Contains rows of items with specific properties (attributes). Lists usually call Procedures.	I,II,III
	TextDisplay	Displays one or more lines of text.	I
	ImageDisplay	Displays pictures.	II
	Slide	Presents a combination of text, images, movies and sound.	II
	FeedbackDisplay	Provides specific feedback based on the participant's response to objects presented earlier in the experiment flow.	II
	MovieDisplay	Displays a movie clip.	III
	SoundOut	Presents a sound file (.wav/.mp3/.wma).	III
	SoundIn	Records sounds.	Not in this book
	Wait	Waits for a specified time without changing the visual output.	III

Icon	Name	Description	Chapter
	InLine	Used to add E-Basic script at a specific location of the experiment flow.	IV
	Label	Indicates a particular location on the timeline (Procedure). The program can 'jump' backward or forward to a Label, in order to repeat or skip a part of the Procedure.	III
	PackageCall	Contains reusable blocks of E-Basic script written by users of E-Prime 2 (often used in Procedures which are used repeatedly or for instance in connecting equipment such as an eye-tracker to an E-Prime® experiment). As packages are beyond the scope of this book, please see the 'E-Prime 2' documentation for a more detailed description.	Not in this book

About the authors

Michiel M. Spapé is a cognitive psychologist at the Helsinki Institute for Information Technology in Finland. Since obtaining his PhD at Leiden University in 2009, he has focused on interrelating the classical functions of the human mind: showing the perception of action, the memory of control, the emotions of problem-solving and the social aspect of individual cognition. Methodologically, he likes to tinker with machines and biology, working with big computers, trackpads, eye trackers, tactors, Kinects, EEG, EMG, MEG and so on. His favourite type of study reheats a venerable psychological effect, spicing it with new tech and adding neuro sauce, before serving it to the academic table.

Rinus G. Verdonschot is trained as a psycholinguist specialized in applied linguistics and cognitive neuroscience. His main work is in in the fields of psycho- and neurolinguistics focusing on language production, reading and bilingualism. He has considerable practical experience working at diverse experimental labs (including EEG/fMRI) in different countries. He enjoys testing theory-driven hypotheses, writing scientific articles about them and presenting the results at international conferences. He also enjoys teaching students at undergraduate and graduate levels and to collaborate with and learn from other researchers.

Saskia van Dantzig was trained as a cognitive psychologist and obtained her PhD on the topic of embodied cognition. She currently works as a senior scientist at Philips Research (Eindhoven, the Netherlands), developing products and services that support people to live a healthy life. She loves to work at the crossroads of psychology and technology, and believes that this combination leads to useful and much needed innovations.

Henk van Steenbergen was trained as an experimental psychologist at Leiden University in the Netherlands where he currently is assistent professor. He likes to combine behavioural, physiological and neuroscientific methods to study human behaviour, in particular the role of emotion and motivation in driving goal-directed action. He was originally educated as an electronic engineer, and so likes to apply cool hardware and software in psychological research. Having been a programmer since his teens, he is convinced that good programming skills enable more efficient and more enjoyable research, a message he tries to convey when teaching E-Prime® programming to graduate students.

Index